A Psychoanalytic Approach to Sexual Difference

Jennifer Yusin

LONDON AND NEW YORK

Designed cover image: © Getty Images

First published 2024
by Routledge
4 Park Square, Milton Park, Abingdon, Oxon OX14 4RN

and by Routledge
605 Third Avenue, New York, NY 10158

Routledge is an imprint of the Taylor & Francis Group, an informa business

© 2024 Jennifer Yusin

The right of Jennifer Yusin to be identified as author of this work has been asserted in accordance with sections 77 and 78 of the Copyright, Designs and Patents Act 1988.

All rights reserved. No part of this book may be reprinted or reproduced or utilised in any form or by any electronic, mechanical, or other means, now known or hereafter invented, including photocopying and recording, or in any information storage or retrieval system, without permission in writing from the publishers.

Trademark notice: Product or corporate names may be trademarks or registered trademarks, and are used only for identification and explanation without intent to infringe.

British Library Cataloguing-in-Publication Data
A catalogue record for this book is available from the British Library

ISBN: 978-1-032-43193-2 (hbk)
ISBN: 978-1-032-43165-9 (pbk)
ISBN: 978-1-003-36609-6 (ebk)

DOI: 10.4324/9781003366096

Typeset in Times New Roman
by Apex CoVantage, LLC

A Psychoanalytic Approach to Sexual Difference

A Psychoanalytic Approach to Sexual Difference analyzes the concepts of sex and gender, showing how sexual difference is characterized by ongoing transformations of spatiality and body, and of essentiality and normativity.

In this book, Jennifer Yusin presents a psychoanalytic study that engages with clinical cases, philosophies of sex and gender, and psychoanalytic writings about sexual difference. She deftly and accessibly analyzes Freud's and Lacan's work on feminine sexuality, Winnicott's notion of the transitional object, and theories of sexuality and gender developed by Judith Butler and Monique Wittig, among others. Yusin starts with the question of how the lack of any essential definition of sexual difference affects subjectivity. She places an emphasis on the psychoanalytic experience and its effects upon how a subject experiences the difference between being a body and having a body. Following Lacan's discovery of the Borromean knot structure of the unconscious and the work of the psychoanalyst Jean-Gérard Bursztein, Yusin continues developing subjective topology as a methodology. She also introduces and shows how sexual difference is linked to transformations of sex and body. Through this, Yusin highlights how it is necessary to reformulate sex, gender, and sexual identities in psychoanalytic theories and in the practice of psychoanalysis. She also speaks to the necessity of generating a new lexicon to help analysts speak about sexual difference in ways that do not perpetuate any essentialism or normativity on the topic.

This book is essential reading for clinicians in psychoanalysis, mental health practitioners in the trans field, and academics working in gender theory, queer and trans studies, and feminist philosophies.

Jennifer Yusin is a psychoanalyst in private practice in Philadelphia, Professor in the Department of English and Philosophy and Director of the Gender and Sexuality Studies Program at Drexel University, USA.

Contents

Preface	*vii*
1 A note about my method: subjective topology	1
2 Some considerations of the changing of psychoanalytic terminology	4
3 On constructing a psychoanalytic lexicon	10
4 Starting points: sex and nomination	14
5 Names-of-the-father: a first approach	18
6 Φ: one sex	20
7 Psychoanalytical invariance	22
8 Some preliminary remarks regarding nomination	25
9 Maternal investment	28
10 Symbolic nomination and redoubling	30
11 The link between speech and nomination	34
12 The difficulty of interpretation	37
13 Signifiers 'man', 'woman': semblant of body	43

vi Contents

14 The psychoanalytical group   46

15 The discourse of the hysteric and jouissance   48

16 All-phallic space/non-all phallic space   51

17 Letters and body   56

18 Signifier and symptom   60

19 Mark in signifier   63

20 Sexual difference: a radical alternative   67

21 Return to a remark in signifier   70

22 Formations of voice   72

23 Fourth consistency   77

24 Assumption of nomination   79

25 A return to our psychoanalytical lexicon   82

    Acknowledgements   *84*
    Bibliography   *85*
    Index   *90*

Preface

Why take up sexual difference today, again? Why take up such a question through a renewal and reformulation of psychoanalytic concepts and theories concerning sex and gender?

The answers here are directly linked to what I owe to clinical experiences, from which—and with great difficulty—I have extracted some lessons that help me build my hypotheses. They are also the lessons that compel me, when a certainty of a knowledge comes, to continuously work on them. When confronted to the task of limiting myself to only a position of a listener, the theoretical assurances that once afforded me feelings of calm were quickly dissolved. By listening, I place an emphasis on the necessity to follow psychoanalytic discourse. Such a discourse compels us to take much different account of things that we think we know such as the physical meaning of our bodies or how language functions. In such encounters, concepts that I once felt sure of understanding lost their consistency. Questions that I thought were solved resurfaced with much more obscurity.

For the psychoanalyst, the encounter with the other—a fellow subject—is a chance to listen that consists in opening oneself to the unknown and of accepting to face perceptions of sufferings and difficulties. I make a distinction between listening and hearing. On the basis of a feminine jouissance, listening implies a capacity to accept and sustain a relation to the unknown. Such an act implies a possibility to hear how the subject of the unconscious is modalizing as a subject of speech, giving substance to a subject's body.[1] That is, there is the possibility to grasp the signifiers that matter for the analysand. Substance is something that is in relation to the statements of a subject. It is close to Aristotle's definition of substance.[2]

I dropped the original aim of this book. Psychoanalytic experience teaches us that there are no easy shortcuts to a 'theory', and further, as Lacan always insisted, the unconscious does not need a theory to operate.[3] My debt to psychoanalytic experience is ongoing. It is thanks to this discourse that my illusions that there might exist a model whose application would no longer confront oddities, incompletions, or errors in logic have broken. I am reminded here of Poincaré's acceptance to face the perceptions linked to the want of a new transformation.[4] It is not easy giving up recourse to a theory, attachments to methodological conventions, or suppositions of knowledge.

It was especially my experiences working with psychosis that forced me to abandon my original aim with this book. This experience, not always easy to accompany and experience subjectively, renders it impossible to cover completely a field of knowledge with the same theory or the same practice. It is sure that a knowledge of sexual difference exists in the psychoanalytic field that can neither be thought nor acted upon by philosophies of sex and gender.

Sexual difference in psychosis is something different than what appears in neurosis. As experience shows, the neurotic holds tightly to a presence of a theoretical model of bisexuality. Current talk among psychoanalytic circles about sexual difference often relies on the idea that a complementarity exists between what might be called a feminine jouissance (or other jouissance) and what I call the jouissance of logos. There exists a knowledge in psychosis that compels us to admit that there are two major modalities of jouissance: neurotic jouissance, which is composed of three types of jouissance, and psychotic jouissance, which is characterized as one consistency. It is true that the neurotic subject thinks such a structure of complementarity exists, and goes looking for it and for ways to be in all the positions offered by it. But it is false in regard to how a subject is marked *as either* 'a woman' *or* 'a man', either as 'boy' or 'girl'. Psychosis does not let us forget that sexual difference does not always appear as a radical alternative for every subject. There are some for whom there is no such alternative. It is impossible to create it ex nihilo.

Hence, my hypothesis: sex is an invention of body. It would be a mistake to think that this hypothesis is a formula. Concerning this hypothesis, I am trying to access and show (as much as possible) how sex is something that is in effect of nomination by establishing a knotting among clinic, theory, and practice. Henceforth, when I say psychoanalytic experience, I am referring to an interlacing of clinic, practice, and theory woven of points known/unknown and of a fundamentally unknowable. The knotting is what gives a certain coherency and consistency to the hypothesis.

As it concerns the question of the clinic and therefore psychoanalytical practice, we can only say that a psychoanalyst's clinic exists. Such a clinic is based on the subjective singularities of a research linked to an analyst's known and unknown knowledge acquired in the experience of the cure. There is no clinic of psychoanalysis such as there is, for example, a medical clinic.[5] In the clinic—there is a demand to limit oneself to occupying only a place of listener. Such a demand is not necessarily there when reading books about psychoanalysis. This teaches us that the object of psychoanalysis cannot be seen. You can only construct it in your subjectivity, in your unknown knowledge, and in your theoretical practice. The object of psychoanalysis is no other than unconscious jouissance in its irreducible singularities.

My interpretations are not claiming to present something new on the topic of sexual difference. This does not make what I say any less risky. My only aim here is consistency and coherency. It goes without saying that one cannot produce any objectivity on the topic of sexual difference. The psychoanalyst is much more comfortable with statements concerning the incompleteness and impossibility inherent in any theory. The philosopher refuses such statements, insisting that there is no sense or knowledge in the real. Psychoanalysis is a different method; it is based on the speaking being and its effects on body and speech.

In saying this, I do not merely wish to emphasize that there exists an irreducible difference between psychoanalytic epistemology (and within this, there is a difference between certainty and knowledge) and the epistemologies coming from the human sciences. I say it because there is no way to avoid the difficulties, obscurities, inconveniences, and incompletions intrinsic to any attempt at a psychoanalytic approach to the subject of sexual difference. Whether this is seen as marked by failures in clarity or errors in logic hardly matters here. If there is no possibility to perceive the clinical thing and the practical implications, then we are, as I grasp it, ipso facto, outside the psychoanalytical field.

I am the first to acknowledge that what I attempt here is far from any conclusion or from providing an exhaustive analysis of the linkage between sex and nomination. I am indebted to my psychoanalytic experience that compelled me to abandon an ideological position. However much entering into a polemic or a critique of what others have said concerning where we are today with sexual difference may satisfy the aesthetic requirements of a theory, it only reiterates what is already known to us.[6]

If these long-winded remarks testify to anything, it is to the impossibility to remove or resolve all difficulties once and for all. It is impossible to avoid our own limitations and constraints in language. One has to choose the option that is, for each one, the necessary condition to carry on. This does not go without acknowledging a symbolic debt in the borrowing of what we have received.

I am aware of the difficulty of my statements, my interpretations, and my descriptions. Today, the increasing prevalence of using inclusive language and the changing of our grammars is a sign of socio-political support for the right of all expressions and identifications of gender and sexuality to exist. It is thanks to the ongoing work of philosophies of sex and gender that we have theories and concepts that help us explain how sex, sexuality, and gender are experienced as a heteronormative power that is lived as a constraint for many persons. These are tremendous advances in our democratic enterprises.[7]

As I grasp it, the recourse to the social as a support for accessing through psychoanalysis a deeper transformation of the differences that torment us—even in the face of the radical injustice of the world—will not change our position. Psychoanalytically speaking, such a subjective transformation is a question of extracting a subjective position linked to an intimate knowledge where the objects that we think appear to us and which presumably guide us to better days no longer worry us.

By now, it may be clear that I am not aiming to build a theoretical knowledge and much less a university discourse. I also hope it is grasped that I am not ignoring or denying that our conceptions of sex and gender are associated to natural objects and cultural objects. I am not seeking to refute the important influences of such associations. I am concerned with questions regarding how a subject comes to a nomination of sex and gender from within their singular, intimate points of subjectivity. I am concerned, more simply, with how sex is existing—with how it is appearing and working for a subject. Sexual life is not the focus.

I know by presenting a psychoanalytic interpretation of sexual difference, I also risk certain suppositions or assessments about where I stand politically and socially on these matters. To try to make a psychoanalytic contribution to these difficult matters that concern everyone, it was necessary to confront the impossibility to say everything. It was necessary for me to limit the field in which I speak and to accept sometimes difficult choices in language. In the effort to try to transmit what psychoanalytic experience teaches us, I proceed without paying attention to the elegance of the presentation or grammatical correctness. Repetitions are inevitable.

For those who take up my hypotheses with another kind of openness, I hope that it will resonate as a preliminary option for an approach to the irreducibility of a subjective position interwoven of what for each one, supports a desire. The hope in the present task is that by not shying away from the long questioning of it, there is the possibility of an ongoing work on the basis of renewable extensions to psychoanalysis.

Notes

1 Subject of the unconscious refers to the formula: a signifier represents a subject for another subject. In the unconscious movement of discourses, the word subject refers to the subject of speech.
2 Aristotle, "Metaphysics," in *The Complete Works of Aristotle 2*, ed. Jonathan Barnes, trans. W. D. Ross (Princeton, NJ: Princeton University Press, 2009).
3 Jacques Lacan, *Television: A Challenge to the Psychoanalytic Establishment*, ed. Joan Copjec, trans. Denis Hollier (New York and London: Norton, 1990).
4 Henri Poincaré, *Science and Method* (New York: Dover Publications, 1952).
5 This is why the passage of the analyst as requiring an institutional guarantee is bound to fail in some regard. There is no one formation of the analyst. There are only ongoing formations of the unconscious.
6 For this reason, it would take us too far from our task to proceed by citation, as is customary in academic discourse and methodology.
7 Some philosophical points relevant to this discussion are to be found in the work of Michel Foucault, Hélène Cixous, Luce Irigaray, Julia Kristeva, Monique Wittig, Gloria Anzaldúa, Judith Butler, Joan Copjec, and Jack Halberstam.

Chapter 1

A note about my method

Subjective topology

Now, generations after Freud and Lacan, psychoanalysis is widespread and mobile. There exists a lot of differences among analysts, psychoanalytical schools, and academic approaches to the field. These differences in style are of no concern here.

In the present task, there is a necessity to make more precise and extend the results of the Freudian and Lacanian discoveries of the subject of the unconscious. This necessity–this way–comes out of research on the topology of the unconscious. Following Lacan's discovery of the topological structure of the unconscious (R, S, I),[1] I work on the open problematic of subjective topology. We owe to the psychoanalyst Jean-Gérard Bursztein the merit of the nomination of subjective topology.[2] We owe to Lacan and Bursztein a change in the status of jouissance and as a result, deeper insight into the spatiality of the unconscious and how it functions. They have shown that psychoanalysis and topology are not two things but one thing moving in a continuous dynamic of transformation. With the discovery of the topological structure of the unconscious, they have uncovered the psychoanalytical concept of nomination. From this, I borrow most of my own subjective topology. If borrowing is to be anything other than a mere repetition of another's thinking, then it must (as I grasp it) involve a psychoanalytic interpretation. More precisely, an interpretation of the subject with regard to jouissance.

Psychoanalytic interpretation neighbors the concept of the cut brought by the mathematician Richard Dedekind. The cut is a nomination of structure, allowing for names designating its spaces.[3] In a subjective topology, the cut has to do with how a signifying movement is generating jouissance.[4] It is also a question of where a formal cut between signifier and jouissance appears. The cut is a way of accounting for how structure is existing as *an unceasing covariation between signifier and jouissance*. It follows the path of necessity. It is not concerned with pointing to something, as if to say, look, here is the necessity, and there is the need. It must be emphasized that structure is a subjective effect. As such, it is covariant with all transformations of jouissance, which are themselves tied to a certain constraint of language.[5] This is why structure can be a synonym for the subject.

This is also why it must be stated that in psychoanalysis, the subject is not an identity, and the body is not an organism. One of the meanings of 'subject' is: *a way of knotting*. Let us not ignore the necessity inscribed into Freud's statement:

DOI: 10.4324/9781003366096-1

2 A note about my method

where the id was, the I has to be.[6] One of the major contributions of Freud's work on neurosis is precisely that there is no *self* in any of the canonical senses of the word. What is called 'self' refers to a division between ideal ego and ego ideal on the basis of an imaginary. There is no way to theorize it with concepts. This point is especially difficult to grasp and admit. Following psychoanalytic discourse, the sayings of analysands that we are asked to listen to have fundamentally different starting points that, it must be admitted, confront us to spaces of appearance where intuition does not serve as a guide.[7]

This is one reason why it is necessary to continuously differentiate an epistemological cut between the consistencies and coherencies of the unconscious field of jouissance and our external, social realities. This alone allows us to get ahold of the irreducibility of our spatial singularities. Formally, this can be summarized by saying that the unconscious has a spatiality and is a space that has no correspondence or resemblance to our usual Euclidean spaces. Although this means that we are compelled to take starting points incommensurable with those having to do with social realities or the real of the world, it also means that we are free from the demand to explain sexual difference through behaviors, the social roles of kinship relations, and other such conducts of reality. This also means that we are once more confronted to the task of deepening the consistency and coherence of the separation between subjective position (what Freud called libidinal position) from conditions of object choice.

A few more remarks. Subjective topology refers to the spatiality of the unconscious in its continuums. It is concerned with space and spatialities realized under forms of the infinite as a fundamental epistemological category in psychoanalysis. Subjective topology is a method and a methodological necessity. It is not a theory made of concepts. It refers to an extraction of a pure element of psychoanalytical knowledge. It is inseparable from the singularity of a psychoanalyst's research in its links to her own unknown knowledge and known knowledge.

Today, there is a lot of confusion regarding Lacan's use of topology. We see this in the proliferation of texts that base themselves on imaginary uses of knots and topological objects. In its visual aspect, the 'knot' is an operator of thought, helping to show how the unconscious is always in a moment of transformation. But topological figures are characterized by an assumption and acceptance of formal constraints. In this sense, they are not drawings, and much less static objects. When I am able, I use topological figures to help transmit what I am able to interpret. As it concerns the emergence of topology in the psychoanalytical field, the thought that psychoanalysis is an implication of mathematical knowledge or that subjective topology is similar to mathematical or philosophical topology misses the fact that the borromean knot is a structure of metaphor. It also misses how it is metaphorizing traces of jouissance. This is not of mere theoretical concern. Clinical consequences follow from such an error, which I try to show at different points.

Psychoanalytic experience obliges us to admit that the impossibility to close meaning is intrinsic to psychoanalytical concepts and theories.[8] Subjective topology is a way of transmitting what of psychoanalytical truth does not pass to the signifier but which in effect, is inseparable from a continuous transformation of space (from movements of jouissance). This is also part of the difficulty of subjective topology. How to make such a linkage—one which is not subjected to external norms but which is only relevant from the experience of the psychoanalytic cure? In a much deeper way, subjective topology helps us reply to the questions about sex and gender that now seem to be troubling sexual difference.

Notes

1 Although Lacan used the term 'subjective topology' early in his work, in his seminar on the *Psychoses*, it took a long time for it to gain a substance. This is why I take as my starting point the moment Lacan discovered the borromean structure of the unconscious (around 1971). It was a real turning point in his work that forced him to start renewing and transforming all of his theories and concepts. Many questions and open problematics have been left for us.

2 From this nomination, Bursztein has uncovered the concepts of consistency and compactification, which have clarified the more obscure functions of jouissance in the ways the unconscious expresses itself. Jean-Gérard Bursztein, *Un lexique de topologie Subjective* (Paris: Hermann, 2017).

3 Richard Dedekind, *Essays on the Theory of Numbers: I. Continuity and Irrational Numbers. II. The Nature and Meaning of Numbers* (New York: Dover Publications, 1963). From the cut, he was able to obtain a definition of the real numbers, and also to name what exceeds the domain of all rational numbers.

4 I emphasize here the subjective function of separation.

5 In Seminar *Ou Pire*, Lacan gets ahold of this when he expresses that there is a correlation between the constraint and what is stirred up by way of passes through speeches. Jacques Lacan, *Or Worse . . . .* ed. Jacques-Alain Miller, trans. A.R. Price, The Seminar of Jacques Lacan, Book XIX (Cambridge: Polity, 2018), 63.

6 Sigmund Freud, "The Ego and the Id," in *The Ego and the Id and Other Works: 1923–1925*, ed. and trans. James Strachey, The Standard Edition of the Complete Psychological Works of Sigmund Freud, vol. 19 (London: Vintage, 2001 [1923]), 1–66.

7 Indeed, psychoanalytical starting points neighbor Aristotle's definition of starting points of substance. There is a difference between a substance and what he calls 'a real thing'. Aristotle, "Metaphysics," 1551–728.

8 Bion's work is particularly illuminating on this point. On the basis of the impossibility to start from a theory or to close a concept, Bion obtains his notion of the psychoanalytical element. Wilfred R. Bion, *Elements of Psychoanalysis* (London: Karnac, 1989).

Chapter 2

Some considerations of the changing of psychoanalytic terminology

We owe to Lacan the merit of naming the existence of the unconscious as a non-being *the real* and *the hole*. These nominations are linked to his discovery of the borromean knot structure of the unconscious. Following this, the situation and place the symbolic and the imaginary occupied in psychoanalytic theory changed. Lacan knew he could no longer rely on the statement: the unconscious is structured like a language.[1] Whereas in his 'early' seminars, the emphasis is on the unconscious and on *being*, the discovery of the equivalence between psychoanalysis and topology allowed him to give a new situation to the real. The knowledge changes. It was a new epistemology he called the *speaking body*.[2] This new object of the unconscious helped him show and develop in a much deeper way how it is characterized by a continuous process of an unfolding of a tridimensionality where the structure inscribes itself. In his work, this is a real turning point that effectively changed the positions of the imaginary, the symbolic, and the real. S, R, I (this was the knotting linked to an emphasis on questions about being) changed to R, S, I (this is the knotting linked to the existence of the unconscious as a question of substance). This is why it is necessary to emphasize the active difference between a topological structure and its spaces of representation.[3]

In this new epistemology, new signifiers emerge. By listening to Lacan, especially in *L'étourdit*, *Ou Pire*, and *Encore*, we can grasp that the symbolic phallus never goes alone. It goes with signifier one (S_1) and with the real. One of the meanings of S_1 is: there is no general foreclosure of the symbolic.[4] The symbolic phallus, S_1, and the real are always present in the transmission of the speech of the maternal Other. He also links the signifiers *substance jouissante* and *signifier one* to the *speaking body*. One definition we can give to the speaking body is: *in every word, the subject speaks*. This implies that S_1 is nothing in itself (this is not the same as saying that it is nothing). But it gives us an idea of what is a substance. This is why the basis of the unconscious is jouissance and why Lacan proposed S_1 as the name of the structure.[5] Let us posit that subjectivity is in a substance that has a jouissance. The difficulty here is to perceive that substance has to do with an inseparability in the composition of matter (signifiers) and a kind of form (jouissance), and with how this inseparability in itself cannot be totalized.

From this, we extract two hypotheses that compelled him to drop the idea that unconscious was only an effect of a signifying network. One is: *language does not*

DOI: 10.4324/9781003366096-2

Some considerations of the changing of psychoanalytic terminology   5

exist. Another is: *there is no speech outside language.*[6] For our purposes here, it is crucial to note that the psychoanalytic truth of what Freud transmitted with what he called *infantile sexuality* is the same in Lacan's epistemology, but the way it is transmitted is different. In consequence of this grasp of a new real (the real of speech), what counts is the symbolic grasp of the body. The implication here may be expressed as follows: the subject of the unconscious is the subject of speech. The unconscious is no longer only the result of a chain of signifiers in which the content was the demand/desire of the Other. This new subject is no other than a subject woven in its jouissances.

This implies a psychoanalytical invariance. *One is an invariance.* There is signifier one (written S_1), which is linked to the ways a subjective structure emerges in reply to experiences of lack. And there is what Freud called *einziger Zug* and what Lacan called *unary trait*. It is the one of repetition (written S_2). Counterintuitive to thought, the status of one as an invariant implies a difference of two that cannot be represented. It does not make a supplementary one. Because of this, it continuously deploys itself into the structure, sexualizing the structure in a trinomial: real, symbolic, and imaginary. These names help explain how the subjective structure works as a one and as the name of the structure by generating concepts.[7] It also helps explain how real, symbolic, and imaginary are also symbolic names that are in effect of a fundamental constraint in language limiting jouissance. Concepts such as symbolic phallus and names-of-the-father help explain how the structure is transmitted from one generation to another under forms of a singular subjective structure.

This is important because it enables us to articulate some of the difficulties relevant from questions of sex and gender to odds and ends of the psychoanalytical experience of the cure. Transference teaches us that a difference of two appears in the enumeration of cuts into signifiers that help the analysand catch a glimpse of their jouissance situation in a fantasy. An analysand relays a dream in which she states, 'it is not my mother'.[8] Here, a simple question of 'really?' from the analyst is sufficient to move a position, a kind of wherefrom I speak as a place that keeps the subject close to the presence of the Other. I am here speaking in the field of neurosis where there is a formal cut between signifier and jouissance. I have found that such a cut does not exist in psychosis. Such an interpretive question goes into the speech of the subject and is enough to enable a moment of subjective change in position. This allows for a glimpse into how, in a fantasy, the subject is making herself into an object for her Other's demands/desires. The subject knows (without wanting to know more about it) that by making herself into the object of the other's dialectical object, she accedes to a cancellation of the subject.[9]

In an experience of a psychoanalytical cure, such cuts into speech slowly and gradually enable a person to get out of an infinite of torment. A clinical translation here is the following: the fall of the transference implies a certain destitution of a pretense of being. By getting ahold of the master signifiers that have a lethal effect and by finding the objects (signifiers of high value) that sustain the subject in her own desires, the analysand knows enough and leaves.[10] She knows how to do with

6 Some considerations of the changing of psychoanalytic terminology

the ways she has been trapped in a fundamental fantasy reducing her to suffering, and no longer needs to transfer it to another. In a way, the love of the Other is changed to a love of one's own symptoms. The subject takes a distance from the Other. Effectively, a space separated from the fundamental fantasy constructed in efforts to complete the Other opens unto possible spaces where extractions of new signifiers and objects enable a subject to step out of desire as the aim. From this, we obtain the following definition of singularity: an irreducible and unsubstitutable difference affirmed in the real of subjectivity.

Because of this, it is no longer sufficient to say that the unconscious is the effect of a signifying chain, induced by the movement of the substitution of the signifiers in the symbolic. There is a necessity to consider the experience of the psychoanalytic cure as an iteration of acts of speech.[11] The moment the speech changes, the jouissance changes. As a result, there is a modification of structure. One of the reasons this is crucial to note is because, as psychoanalytic experience shows, the Other has only two major modalities of existence: symbolic and imaginary. The Other is a gaze that is always looking, introducing the subject to two instances: the ideal ego and an ego ideal.[12] The truth has no signifier. This is how I interpret there is 'no other of the other'.

It seems to me that there is a particular danger in much of the texts about psychoanalysis. This is tied to our experiences of words and concepts. Many of the words and concepts that psychoanalysis uses cannot elide the fact that they meet with histories of ideas, deeply held associations to already given meanings, long standing uses in other fields, and assumptions that they belong to other discourses. This seems especially the case with the word *symbolic*. Especially when authors swept up by Lacanian inspiration are writing about the symbolic, it becomes very hard to grasp what they are referring to (to mathematical language, the functional power of language, written symbols and signs, etc.). I have often had the impression that this is especially the case when there is an attempt to specify the relation between the signifier of the phallus and the phallus. This highlights a real difficulty, from which I continuously work to extract myself.

What concerns me more is the use of the imaginary, which plays a very great deal in the abuses of language that we find in such attempts at the symbolic. This point is not easy to describe with precision. I can say that it is linked to the idea of the variability of the imaginary. Underlying the idea of the imaginary is a certain pretense of thought. We think we can know all variations as a knowledge possessed once and for all. It is a kind of forcing of the lack into being a supreme element of change. In unfolding infinite horizons, such a thought conceals a wish to maintain at all costs a notion of unlimited possibility for the development of the individual as essentially a constituent of the universal.[13] This also gets at a very deep difficulty, which has precisely to do with what psychoanalysis calls the object. The object *is condition and cause*.

It is not easy to accept that lack is not in itself an element. It is not a thing, and much less an entity. What gives it its function of cause is its situation in a fantasy. This is relevant from the subjective grasp of the link between where the object is situated (in act and in potential) and how it is appearing in spaces of representation (outside-object) that can be fulfilled by an emptiness or a function. Following this, it becomes possible for the subject to name experiences of something missing or lacking by naming its affective and persistent dependence on these privations. This is why the object is realized either as an object fantasized as a partialized object of impulses (voice, breast, excrement, gaze) or as an object referring to the symbolic value of the phallus. The important point here is that naming is inseparable from how a subject finds and puts equivalences to a lack that fundamentally cannot be reconstituted or retrieved. This gives a consistency to the feeling of there being something that can fulfill or overcome the confrontation to an experience of non-equivalence.

In the effort to reduce, as much as is possible, the effects of these difficulties, I prefer to give a sense of how I deploy and define the real, the symbolic, and the imaginary. I emphasize that I have obtained these definitions as a result of what I have learned so far about the ways the unconscious is existing. It is therefore necessary to state that the existence of the unconscious implies that it is a modal real, realized in act or in potential. As a result, the unconscious is differentiated in itself from within its internal knottings through three modes of existence: the real of the real, the real of the symbolic, and the real of the imaginary.

Let us posit that in a fundamental way, the real is unreachable; it cannot be touched. It is in this sense that the real makes a hole; it is not merely denoting the category of the impossible. It introduces the impossible as a necessary condition for the existence of a space separated from one's own, and for something coming from a space that is *heteros* to it in order to incorporate it into material that is homogenous with its structure.[14] Here, one finds a resonance with Lacan's calling of the real as what *ek-sists* to the subject and truth, the *sister* of jouissance.[15] This is a necessary process, one that may here be called the necessity to construct one's own borromean knot (that is, a fantasy), implying an ongoing process of resituating jouissance. One of the meanings of this is the necessity to construct *a fantasy* separated from parental fantasies. Freud's essay 'A Child is Being Beaten' is particularly illuminating in regard to this necessity. At issue is the need for the child to continuously make extractions of signifiers that will come to constitute her unconscious arrangement of signifiers, allowing the unconscious to represent to itself what it wishes to recollect of its 'own' experience. Because of this, I am also calling the real of the subject *a knot*.

The *real of the real* refers to the suffering and torment of the subject, which is felt beyond all meaning, representation, and imagination. It is linked to variations of jouissance, including its absences/presences and its retroactions. It is also the structure as one.

The *real of the symbolic* refers to a hole in knowledge implying the real existence of the lack in being. It also has to do with the emergence of elements of lack (marks) that the subject uses to make the existence of the law coherent with its own structure.

The *real of the imaginary* refers to an unconscious image of narcissism situating a consistency that gives materiality to objects denoting the construction of a reality. It is also what gives consistency to identification.

8 Some considerations of the changing of psychoanalytic terminology

This allows us to state that the real, the symbolic, and the imaginary are also signifying elements metaphorizing each other in the way we represent the subject we are, from within spaces of representation. It is in this sense that that we can say *they are like dimensions of space*. It is more precise to say that they are consistencies. As I will try to show, this helps us situate ourselves more precisely with regard to how the subject of sex is extending itself in a finality aiming at a knotting of the different consistencies one by one.[16] Let us also therefore state that the knot is a principle of an internal finality.[17] The topological structure of the unconscious is written as (R, S, I). As elements that support each other in their differentiations, these consistencies are written as (R), (S), (I). When I write the words real, symbolic, or imaginary, it is because in that moment, it is to help differentiate between signifier and letter on the basis of an interpretation of jouissance. I will try to explain this difference.

Notes

1 This does not imply that there is a negation of his earlier formulations of psychoanalytical theories and concepts. It is rather to do with an unknotting and knotting of known and unknown points enabling the emergence of new concepts that help us speak about the unconscious in more precise ways. The term *sexuation* helps since, from the point of view of the speaking subject, it henceforth obliges us to take account of extensions of jouissance (R), (S), (I).

2 From Seminar *Encore*: 'An opening, by which it is the world that makes us into its partner, is created thereby. It is the speaking body' (120). 'The real, I will say, is the mystery of the speaking body, the mystery of the unconscious' (131). Jacques Lacan, *On Feminine Sexuality: The Limits of Love and Knowledge*, ed. Jacques-Alain Miller, trans. Bruce Fink, The Seminar of Jacques Lacan, Book XX (New York: W. W. Norton & Company, 1999).

3 This also helps explain why it is necessary to grasp the formal constraints inherent to deploying topological figures in a psychoanalytic description. Clinically speaking, missing the active difference can lead to assumptions that the sinthome is a supplement created by an analytic experience. It misses the question of how (R), (S), (I) are already there, existing as an infinite of elements. This is why Lacan never answers the question, was Joyce mad?

4 It is therefore not true, as some state, that the Other no longer exists. Such a statement is relevant from a socio-political point of view.

5 Lacan, *Or Worse . . . .*

6 This is close to what Wittgenstein developed in his philosophy in the *Tractatus Logico-Philosophicus*. It is not a question of the meaning of language but how one uses language. 'Objects I can only name. Signs represent them. I can only speak of them. I cannot assert them. A proposition can only say how a thing is, not what it is' (38). Ludwig Wittgenstein, *Tractatus Logico-Philosophicus*, trans. C. K. Ogden (Mineola: Dover Publications, 1999).

7 One notices that this is how we come to experience concepts. Ideas like variable names enable us to experience relations to meanings of words.

8 Freud's essay on negation is illuminating on this point. The 'not a' is equal to the truth of 'a'. It is sufficient to invoke a repression to know that what has situated outside (not-a) will in some way return as different to itself. Sigmund Freud, "Negation," in *The Ego and the ID and Other Works: 1923–1925*, ed. and trans. James Strachey, The Standard

Edition of the Complete Psychological Works of Sigmund Freud, vol. 19 (London: Vintage, 2001 [1925]), 233–40.

9 As Ludwig Jekels shows in "Psychoanalysis and Dialectic", there is no leap from psychoanalysis to the dialectic. Because of the non-existence of the Other, 'dialectic' is forced in an imaginary way. Ludwig Jekels, "Psycho-Analysis and Dialectic," *Psychoanalytic Review* 28 (1941): 228–53.

10 Lacan tried to formalize this with the help of the formulation *des-être* (implying a subjective destitution).

11 This compels us to give up ideas of 'endings' and 'beginnings' in psychoanalysis. How to conceptualize the moment of the conclusion of an encounter between analyst and analysand is a necessary question. Doing so, important as it is, would take us too far away from our immediate concerns in this essay. I must therefore put it to the side.

12 Jacques Lacan, *The Four Fundamental Concepts of Psychoanalysis*, ed. Jacques-Alain Miller, trans. Alan Sheridan, The Seminar of Jacques Lacan, Book XI (New York: W. W. Norton & Company, 1998).

13 I am of the opinion that philosophies that build their critiques of psychoanalytic approaches to subjective phenomena on the basis of the law of negation remain blind to certain fundamental points acquired in the psychoanalytic experience, where especially the clinic teaches us that there is no abstract universal that can be deduced from experience. Even if it should appear that there are unknown attributes between the intellect (or the mind or spirit) and the body, there is no third term (a 'force'), which functions as ontological proof of psychoanalysis as a kind of sociological doctrine. We are obliged by certain facts of subjective existence that come from lessons in clinical experience to bring down from the heights of the dialectic, the concepts of change and imaginary. In a certain way, psychoanalysis is a method incommensurable with the scientific methodology at the base of dialectical constructions.

14 Hole is a concept borrowed from topology. It means: there are no common elements between inside and outside. From Seminar *R.S.I.*: 'The number 3 is to demonstrate what it is if it is the Real, namely the Impossible, it is the most difficult kind of demonstrations ... it must be impossible, a condition required for the real' (170). Lacan takes back the term *heteros* from antiquity and renews it. Jacques Lacan, "Seminar XXII: RSI," trans. Cormac Gallagher, 1974–75 (unpublished).

15 Session IV from Seminar *The Other Side of Psychoanalysis*; and in Seminar *Encore*, he states jouissance is '*ek-sister au dit*' (22). Jacques Lacan, *The Other Side of Psychoanalysis*, ed. Jacques-Alain Miller, trans. Russell Grigg, The Seminar of Jacques Lacan, Book XVII (New York: W. W. Norton & Company, 2007). Lacan, *On Feminine Sexuality: The Limits of Love and Knowledge.*

16 We owe to Bursztein the nomination of consistency. Jean-Gérard Bursztein, *Psychanalyse et Philosophie Borroméenne* (Paris: Hermann, 2019).

17 On the basis of four fundamental operations relevant from the phallic function, this internal finality is a knot to three. I associate these operations to: listening, writing, speaking, and language. They constitute the psychoanalytic operation as relevant from interpretive cuts linked to forms of voice.

Chapter 3

On constructing a psychoanalytic lexicon

Everyday experience teaches us that coincident with the growth of an infant into a toddler, the young subject acquires the faculties of speech and language while learning how to use them in concert with attaining various stages of independence. To these activities we associate processes called 'self-discovery', 'development', 'weaning', 'sleep training', and so forth. Even given the abundance of phrases used to describe this, everyone knows that what is involved are sets and series of interactions with the young subject aimed at ensuring life and its continued independent growth and progress. It is precisely these sorts of objective aims, continuously influenced by social pressures and roles, assumptions as to what makes for 'good' or 'bad' parents, assessments as to when a child should be 'speaking' with varying levels of linguistic competencies, etc., that have no place in psychoanalytic interpretations.

Psychoanalytic experience teaches us that it is impossible to deduce any kind of universal that can be applied with a view to patterns (whether generally or particularly). It also teaches us that however much representations of affects may conform to what we perceive as corresponding to the experiences of others, there is no way to know or say more about such temporal successions. This has to do with one of Freud's deeper and indeed more enigmatic discoveries regarding the unconscious as relevant from deletions of time.[1]

It is true that social dynamics (conceived as they are by human sciences) and parental idiosyncrasies experienced in the life of an individual serve to represent the complexity of how we come to construct and unfold subjectivity. In this sense, it speaks to an overdetermination of the subject, which no doubt plays a powerful role in the fantasy of a group. I would like to emphasize the following: assertions concerning the unconscious as born of culture, as inherently social in the sociological sense, or as a modern, philosophical subject in the sense that it is constituted by discursive redistributions of 'power' amount to saying that only some have an unconscious or that there is only one analytic formation. Here, the unconscious is falsely thought, even though these are not false pretenses running through such a thinking.

This is necessary to clarify because speaking about psychoanalytic phenomena with precision and without deviating from our field is an ongoing work inseparable

DOI: 10.4324/9781003366096-3

On constructing a psychoanalytic lexicon 11

from our present task. I mean here to emphasize something that comes from the encounter with an other in the experience of transference. There is no need, for example, to say the word 'unconscious' when working with an analysand. The presence of a word experienced as imposed and full of authority can have an alienating effect on the analysand, which can evoke a wish to murder, generating more guilt. This implies two other necessities. We must arrive at a gap in order to make common references. We must also keep certain (some, not all) references because of how they function in the subjective acceptance or refusal of the law of castration. As I grasp it here, we cannot get outside of language. One has to recognize, however, that when the subject comes to speech, it is impossible to say everything all at once or to put all the jouissance into the structure. The fundamental lack in language is something different than something ineffable.

We are thus faced with the ever-present task of a continuous building and changing of a lexicon. It is not easy because the assumptions and meanings of psychoanalytical concepts can never be closed.[2] Contrary to common intuition, such a development is not a matter of understanding fundamental definitions or of merely satisfying a want of definition by using linguistics to make distinctions. By the term 'lexicon', I mean an ongoing process that helps us deepen our knowledge of what we call the unconscious. This implies obtaining definitions that compel us to change and refine our terminology and descriptions, in an effort to give them new meaning and speak about our topic in increasingly more precise ways.[3] This is another way of knotting the subject. Following the real as a covariation between structure and jouissance, I would say that such work proceeds by a principle of weaving extractions of elements of psychoanalytic knowledge together with formalism. This means that the knowledge it presents is always provisional, always to be reformulated.

Because such work is connected to the ways each psychoanalyst ties intimate truth to a subjective knowledge, psychoanalytic terminology is marked by a certain counterintuitivity of thought and is contrary to the common usage of words. Indeed, it is in this sense that psychoanalysis is the other of the social.

I propose to take as starting points the following terms and definitions that I have been able to extract and am able to interpret:

subject: a way of knotting the structure. Another word for subject is structure. Only subject effects exist for which the objective existence of a subject is not necessary *a priori*.

signifier: bearer of jouissance, in act or in potential. Signifiers are what the subject thinks, on the basis of a supposition of a lack and a perception of it, are the objects of the Other's demand/desire. It is not a linguistic unit or entity.

jouissance: a compact space. It is a knowledge seized by the subjective body as a perception. There is no intellectual conception of it.

12 On constructing a psychoanalytic lexicon

letter: an effect of speech. They are statements of a presence of a jouissance that has been lost. Letters are linked to an instantiation of a signifier and, thus, to a call to resituate jouissance. As such, they echo a missing jouissance in the structure in metaphorizing the real external to the subject. Letters are therefore also metaphorized in the signifying elements of the symbolic, which are themselves metaphorized in the representations of the imaginary. Letters cannot be imagined or fantasized; they are felt without object.

semblant: helps us designate spaces of appearance. One of the meanings of semblant is that signifiers induce a reality. Within the speech of the subject, there exists a certain number of signifiers that designate the appearance of the objects of reality. Such appearances are fluctuating moments of the appearance of things. Because speech does not aim at being but at *seeming*, the 'semblant' is concerned with interrelations between jouissance and signifiers. It is inseparable from the difference between jouissance and signifier as expressing the real of the subject.

metaphor: a modality of speech expressing an impossible to say, felt beyond all meaning, and which cannot be said otherwise. Metaphorization is a process made on the basis of substitutions in a signifying chain. It continuously infers and exposes the fiction of language. It is not a production of the imagination.

mother: agent of nomination and variable. It is equivalent to being.

paternal function: the function of the father is the function of naming. Function is an effect of a cut or a separation. Speaking of the function of naming gives a substance to the names-of-the-father.

names-of-the-father: signifiers of high value. It is an element that can function as a suture. It is also not a pure belief in the holy father. It refers to a belief in something we call the law. The symbolic father is a reference (an *ek-sistence*), which is also something that is introduced to the law.

the Other: the place where one speaks with a signifier. The subject of speech is one spoken by the Other. This implies that for every subject, there exists an irreducibility linked to the Other's double, modal existence implied in language. This double (absence/presence) is indexed to two modalities: it exists with signifiers of demands where there is the cancellation of the subject; it exists with signifiers of desire that make the existence of the subject more and more probable.

It is important to emphasize that psychoanalysis aims at helping to make the effect of a separation from the perceived demands of the Other, the possible place from which one can extract the signifiers that support a strength and stability in desire beyond durability. A real difficulty of psychoanalytical work has to do with supporting a subject not only in the extraction of new signifiers, which goes with realizing the signifiers that generate a lethal suffering. It also has to do with realizing a capacity to situate new signifiers in the places where the experience of a lack is otherwise felt as unbearable and intolerable, that is, in the spaces empty of jouissance. It is not a matter of handing interpretations to the analysand but of helping the analysand in making her own interpretations through methodological singularities. This is why a necessary condition of transference is also taking into account the analyst's desires. I have found that the psychotic subject especially insists upon this necessity. This is why the analyst must also take seriously her or his position as a semblant.

It is the inseparability of the work of extracting, realizing, and giving a new situation to a set of signifiers that the existence of a singular desire is an effect more and more probable for the subject. In this way, it is one that is increasingly consistent in its separations from the demands/desires of the Other. It is in this sense that we may speak of desire as having to do with a certainty of knowing *to one's own eyes* that one is a subject of value. This is also why it is necessary to accept that desire cannot be created out of nothing. Such work—which is very difficult because it also implies an acceptance to lose an unconscious image of suffering or glory—allows the subject to stand in her or his own desire. To put it more formally, desire is no longer the metonymy of a lack-to-be. It is no longer the ultimate object. Desire consists in a transformation of jouissance linked to changes in position of new signifiers. Desire moves to support the substantial existence of a subject in her or his irreducible subjectivity.

Notes

1 This is what Freud called *die endliche und die unendliche analyse* (analysis finite and infinite). This has been unfortunately translated as analysis terminable and interminable. Freud, Sigmund. (1937). Analysis Terminable and Interminable." in *Moses and Monotheism: An Outline of Psycho-Analysis and Other Works: (1937–1939)*, edited and translated by James Strachey, 209–54. The Standard Edition of the Complete Psychological Works of Sigmund Freud, vol. 23. (London: Vintage, 2001).
2 Burzstein's contributions to our psychoanalytical lexicon through a subjective topology leads to significant values in its ongoing development.
3 Here one can grasp the resonances of borrowing as acknowledging a symbolic debt. It also comes close to Aristotle and the idea that definition is a reply to a why, not a what.

Chapter 4

Starting points

Sex and nomination

It is well-known that a difference between what in everyday language is called 'man' or 'woman' exists. Inquiries as to the nature, functioning, and meanings of these differences are intimately tied to our experiences, especially to experiences of our bodies. Psychoanalysis sheds light on the fact that the ways the subject deploys such a difference cannot be explained by anatomical differences or by cultural commands, even though there is plenty of material that suggests otherwise.

How does a subject come to unconsciously make use of what appears to be 'the other sex' and designate himself or herself as 'a boy' or as 'a girl'? However much a subject's experiences and speech appear to us as arranged in agreement with external, social norms (even if they are in agreement with modes of resistance against norms experienced as oppressive constraints), the unconscious nomination of the subject does not tally with the socio-cultural organization of sex and gender as attributes of social modes, sexual practices, and sets of behaviors. We observe further that for the neurotic subject, the difference between 'woman'/'man' appears as a radical alternative that the subject thinks she can either avoid or divert through a fantasy.[1] For the psychotic subject, such a difference does not appear as a radical alternative. The difference appears more like a radix deployed at most in one.

What this means may be expressed as follows: there is no part in common between the two substances called 'woman' or 'man' in language. Contrary to what is thought, this difference of two does not produce another one. It is only one. In a fundamental way, such a one is not deducible from a universe of ideas. Paradoxical as this assertion may appear, this one is not born of the same reasoning that guides us to operations called antimonies. It is true, as the discourse of hysteria teaches us, that a relation between a subject's unconscious content and how a subject partakes of logic becomes apparent through the transference. But man's eternal contemplation of the navel of his dream is not the object of psychoanalysis. That it touches nature, and one day or another comes into contact with it, does not provide us with a sufficient basis for explaining how this alterity is put into place for a subject. We are obliged to follow psychoanalytic discourse. Regarding our subject, we learn that conducts of reality do not sufficiently explain deeper, innermost experiences of sex and gender. This is why it is necessary to shake off purely verbal definitions and to no longer content ourselves with words.

DOI: 10.4324/9781003366096-4

I have thus set myself the task of trying to explain *unconscious nomination*. There is a relation between sex and what the subject takes as an assignation to a gender. Contrary to philosophical or sociological approaches to the topic, we find that such a relation is in effect of the continuous speech of the mother. Upon giving up the idea that nomination is a sociological call, we can make a more precise statement. The way the subject will call himself or herself 'a man' or 'a woman' is in reply to an imperative to be situated in an all-phallic space or in a non-all phallic space. Because of this, the way we fantasize the kind of subject we are is through a fantasy of a gender. I will restate my earlier hypothesis. Sex is an invention of body. I add the hypothesis that body and gender are covariant with respect to the ways the subject of speech passes into language.

By pass into language, I mean this: the subject is compelled to be a subject. In reply, the subject makes spatial operations. The subject extracts signifiers and objects in reply to the necessity to subjectivize the structure by a lack. This has to do with the fundamental need of the subject to designate himself or herself as a subject from within a double structure of speech.[2] Let us recall earlier hypotheses: *language does not exist*, and *there is no speech outside language*. I emphasize that these two hypotheses go together. It is not a question of one occurring and then the other. For example, it is not precisely a matter of a kind of shaping of an experience the subject is aware of (or is coming into awareness of) by naming a feeling.

I am not here describing this necessity to name as situated in the place where the subject identifies an affective experience to a feeling. This activity of naming feelings is no doubt important and must not be ignored or denied. But it has do with inducing a specular complementarity to satisfy the inability to reconstitute a lost 'original' presence that marks the subject's body. In neurosis, this complementarity works like an equivalence by inducing an incessant play of absence/presence. Such a specular complementarity consists in grasping the fact that there is no direct intuition of the distance from the other body. This helps explain why the imaginary must be considered like a dimension around which is extended a real of subjectivity.

Let me try to situate the difficulty regarding my starting points on sex and nomination with regard to the real. The necessity of which I speak has to do with naming as having the effect of making an addition of dimension in the subjectivity of a subject.[3] It is not merely limited, for example, to an imaginary or to the symbolic. *Nomination is a process of necessary privation.* On the basis of something that fundamentally cannot be experienced by the subject, it will come to constitute the ways a subject will construct and put into place a subjective body. It is a question of how castration is transmitted from one generation to another. Nomination brings us to a question of the difference between the real and words linked to the non-equivalence of sex to any sort of being.[4]

Confronted to this difference, the subject is compelled to extract an infinite of signifiers that help put an equivalence to something felt like a missing fusion and which continues to call for it. I associate this necessity to close a space to *the necessity to close the sentence*.[5] More precisely, I mean a simple statement of the subject. To this, I further associate the process of compactifying the space, which

16 Starting points

brings about the meaning and sense effects. Such a process is always iterating itself as different to itself. It is by a feeling of a lack that the subject will subjectivize her passes into language. Signifiers are not in themselves the equivalents. They come out of missing something felt like a fusion, which immediately calls for an equivalence to satisfy it. In effect, they help the subject perceive causality (object). The following figure helps show this:

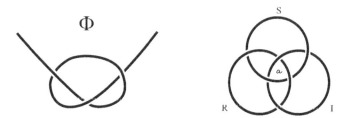

Let us recall that in the case of the Wolf Man, the moment he gets ahold of the signifier груша (grusha), there is an immediate induction of jouissance evoking a lacking whole (a presence of a fusional one).[6] The evocation of a first love (a maternal love) induced by the name груша is linked to the wish to have the love of the father. In this way, груша is also a renunciation of a lack in an imaginary object. This renunciation is in effect a substituting of the phallic one to the one of sex. This substitution generates a source of sense; груша takes the place of the sexual that lacks.

For the psychoanalyst, the equivalence is where the conceptualization of a separated being appears in revealing the nonexistence of such a relation with the one. Such a relation, which is a kind of fusion of body in a unity, is what psychoanalysis calls the sexual relation. Eros names one of the ways this nonexistence radically affects the structure. Elsewhere, it is called *being*. This process of generating equivalencies on the basis of *a missing jouissance* never stops differentiating itself from within the three consistencies we call (R), (S), (I).[7] It is important to emphasize that compactifying the space does not always result in separated consistencies in which each one supports the other (such as in the case of psychosis).

Underlying Lacan's discovery of the borromean structure of the unconscious is the necessity of a fourth term. It seems that nomination is characterized by a continuous deployment of names/names-of-the-father, and that this deployment supports how the unconscious is existing.[8] The knottings of the subject show that the emergence of the structure of the unconscious is always referring to an ungraspable real. This means that knottings of the subject are unconscious situations of jouissance.

Notes

1 This helps explain why there is often a reliance of explaining sexual difference in the psychoanalytical field through the idea of bisexuality. Sometimes this idea is expressed through a notion of a complementarity between fields of jouissance.
2 Bursztein makes this point precise by showing the interrelation between the moebian structure of the unconscious and the borromean structure of the unconscious. Bursztein, *Un lexique de topologie Subjective*.

Starting points   17

3 This neighbors what Saul Kripke develops with respect to simple sentences in *Naming and Necessity*. Saul A. Kripke, *Naming and Necessity* (Cambridge: Harvard University Press, 1980).

4 It is where the nonexistence of the sexual relation is revealed. There is an insuperable hiatus between this starting point and the activity of starting from a place that rests on equivocations of being.

5 This necessity to close the sentence is written into the borromean structure (R, S, I), which is that of the necessity to close a space called (a).

6 Sigmund Freud, "From the History of an Infantile Neurosis." in *An Infantile Neurosis and Other Works: 1917–1919*, ed. and trans. James Strachey, The Standard Edition of the Complete Psychological Works of Sigmund Freud, vol. 17 (London: Vintage, 2001 [1918]), 1–124.

7 This is hard to explain. This is what I grasp Lacan was trying to show regarding the infinite of the void through the conceptualization of the *asphère* in *L'étourdit*. It neighbors the linkage between what Aristotle laid down with regard to the mathematical object in Book IV of *Physics*, as well as the continuous process of opening and closing the sphere of speech in *On Marvelous Things Heard*. This touches upon how accustomed we are to thinking that we can represent to ourselves thought as a succession of spaces. It is a kind of syllogistic thinking that supposes our reflections on space in some way mirror our past spaces. From this, we obtain a simple representation of the equivalence (written as =). On the basis of conventions in logic, we are justified in our reasons for this. It is an affirmation of the mind, which knows it can, once an act is possible, henceforth conceive of an indefinite repetition of the same act. Indeed, it is even more helpful that this mathematical object (interpreted as to its function as a sign or symbol) is taken to be axiomatic since this allows us to make infinitely many statements regarding representations and meanings of different types of relations, as well as functions of relations. However, one cannot help that in the moment of saying something by naming it, one realizes a formal apophantic. Aristotle, "On Marvellous Things Heard," in *The Complete Works of Aristotle 2*, ed. Jonathan Barnes, trans. L. D. Dowdall (Princeton: Princeton University Press, 2009), 1272–98; Aristotle, "Physics," in *The Complete Works of Aristotle 1*, ed. Jonathan Barnes, trans. R. P. Hardie and R. K. Gaye (Princeton: Princeton University Press, 2009), 315–446; Jacques Lacan, "L'étourdit," in *Autres Écrits*, Le Champ Freudien (Paris: Editions du Seuil, 2001), 449–95.

8 To help express the inseparability of unknotting and knotting and the effects of generating a dynamic of structure, I use the word *deployment*.

Chapter 5

Names-of-the-father

A first approach

Even if the terms 'signifier' and 'jouissance' are not used by Freud, Lacan shows that they are already in Freud's discourse, in the place of privilege given to myth as a necessary condition for thinking the origin of structure. In *Moses and Monotheism*, Freud makes precise the fact that we start from an idea of the father in order to arrive at a notion of supreme being, which one may call 'god'. In *Totem and Taboo*, Freud once more points to the fact that the subject starts from an idea of the father, adding that this idea consists in thinking that he has all the women. In *Totem and Taboo*, he shows that the law of the prohibition of incest only exists through a series of statements that the group interprets as to the presence of foundational statements supposed to the group.

The series of statements enunciated by law of the prohibition of incest (for example, no son can copulate with his mother), suppose that such statements cannot be self-created out of nothing. The logical systems that coordinate the existence of a subject as something which carries on, as something perceived as a living being, as having a value for others, and so forth, requires the adherence to signifiers that function as authoritative names. What Freud discovered, and what Lacan makes more precise, is that the law of the prohibition of incest (the law of the unconscious) must take *the form of sexual difference.*[1]

This is where Lacan takes us steps further with the concept of the names-of-the-father. He finds that the obligation to follow the law turns following the supposition of a lack indexed to two major modalities: the belief in the father as existence and the adherence to the authoritative of names. He shows that Freud needed to think the existence of the unconscious on the basis of a coextension between the mythical element of the murder of the father and the generation of the law in order to soothe the guilt of the filial assassins. The law of the prohibition of incest actualizes itself as a symbolic law. In the Oedipus complex, Lacan designates the fact of *the necessity to hypothesize the existence of the structure*. In the unconscious discourses of the subject, the signifier 'father' emerges jointly with that of the mother's speech. This obliges one to open a space different to an imaginary genealogy and to think the existence of the subject.

Let us notice that one of Lacan's logical writings of the law, $\exists x \, \overline{\Phi x}$, implies the possibility of a contingent encounter in which the subject is obliged to have a

DOI: 10.4324/9781003366096-5

value for others that is different to the one supposed to the idea of the father. What comes into subjective existence by the statement, 'there exists one for whom the phallic function does not work', is another implied statement. This statement is a proposition characterized by the fact not all propositions must be true and/or false.[2] Because of this, there must be a symbolic nomination. Without it, there can be no way for the subject to find in the body of a radically different other an equivalence of the lost presence of the father and the mother. The difficulty here is to perceive and grasp that the unconscious is not conditioned by any conscious processes or awareness.

Let us also note that the jouissance supposed to the signifier 'father' in 'there exists one' is that of an absolute, unlimited jouissance. It is not easy to perceive that by 'absolute jouissance', we must also admit the existence of a knowledge about which one cannot speak.[3] It assumes the presence of a statement that refers the child to a meaning and a place she cannot in any way assume. The price we pay for this supposition of a lack in *knowledge of cause* is that the signifier 'father' is devoid of meaning. But because it must still have some sense, it also, no doubt, means the existence of a subject alone in the world, and of which nothing is asserted, and which cannot involve contradiction. One can only say that it is subjected to incompleteness, and the subject must embody, through metaphor, a new living name. One of the meanings of what Freud called a forced choice is the necessity to introduce a referent *in order* for the possibility of difference to flourish.

For Lacan, the *necessity to hypothesize the existence of the structure* implies a fiction to be discarded. This fiction—linked to the fact that at bottom, the Oedipus complex is formed of a myth of man and woman—is no other than that of language. It is within the continuous inference of such a fiction that the subject persists in the false thought that the phallus has a content or representation in itself. Such a thought keeps one believing that the 'law' tying 'woman'/'man' is founded on a structural complementarity of jouissance.

Notes

1 Psychoanalysis defines incest as a subject's attempt to merge or fuse with the Other in a fantasy. It is not defined by kinship roles or behaviors among individuals in families. To grasp this, it is necessary to follow that incest is situated in the transmission of structure from one generation to another. This is how, in a way counterintuitive to thought, Freud was able to perceive that incest is inseparable from the thing, and that its first move is from the child to the mother.
2 In other words, it is a statement of the subject which does not have to be true or is lacking in being true ('being true' is a semantic characteristic).
3 This neighbors Wittgenstein's statement in the *Tractatus Logico-Philosophicus*: 'whereof one cannot speak thereof one must be silent' (27).

Chapter 6

One sex

The difficulty here is to try to hypothesize how the difference between jouissance linked to 'man' and jouissance linked to 'woman' exists for the subject without any presence. Because such a difference has no consistence in itself, and is irreducible in a fundamental way, there is no intellectual conception of it. Having no other recourse to a knowledge of it, this irreducibility remains only as something that the subject is compelled to organize into a logic comprised of two major modalities of difference: a logic of contradictory difference (or opposites) and a logic of difference as diversities.[1] This is what Freud called *unterschied* and *verschiedenheit*.

We should take seriously the fact that neither Freud nor Lacan could say what such a difference is made of. In his writings on femininity and feminine sexuality, Freud said that there is a libido and that it is a kind of sexual strength. With this, he also said something that is repeated throughout his work. He says that he cannot give any content to this libido. Lacan picks up on the fact that this point of no analysis in Freud never goes without 'one'. For example, there is one phallic phase, there is one libido.[2]

In Seminars *Ou Pire* and *Encore*, Lacan presents a very precise study of Freud's work on femininity by articulating it to his theory of unconscious sexuation. In these seminars, we can see that he is trying to explain this point of no analysis with the phallic function and the difference between structure and signifier one. What Freud calls libido is what Lacan will call the phallic function. It is a reformulation of sexuality. It is also a moment when he grasps that topology is a way to explain how something is working without access to causal determinations. He also says something that is complicated to grasp and interpret.

He is sure that there is a difference between man/woman, but still, on no account can he say what this difference is made of.[3] This difference exists, but it has no signifier that determines it. We are, as it were, expelled from this point of saying more about it. This situation of a point from which we are expelled is what Lacan will call the *phallus*. One of the meanings of this is that we belong to the same space. How we participate in this space and how we access the lack in signifier and in the 'other sex' is something felt per each subject's imaginary. It is not all the same for every subject. The only way that we can try to say something of this other relation is to try to interpret it by metaphorizing jouissance, with the help of *letters*. This

DOI: 10.4324/9781003366096-6

jouissance linked to letters has an effect of body without signifying an objective genitive. It is indeed like a mystical point in analysis.

What Lacan calls *discourse* refers to the logical modalities of the encounter with the Other through which the subject passes.[4] This differentiates what he calls sexuation from sexuality. In his matheme for sexuation,[5] we can extract that $\cancel{La}$ expresses the impossibility to give a content to the phallus. Because of this, the vectors differentiate the ways the subject fantasizes the Other and, thus, the ways the subject of the unconscious is flattened out either as 'man' or as 'woman'. 'Man' is where the subject is a substance situating the paternal function. It is written: $\exists x \, \overline{\Phi x}$ (the one who says no to incest). 'Woman' is where $\cancel{La}$ situates not merely the lack-in-being, but a lack in jouissance.

From these points of no-analysis, we can also extract that *there is one sex*. For every subject, there is a point that cannot be grasped and about which it is not possible to say more.[6] This is one of the meanings of 'there is one sex'. This point of real modalized as impossible is written with the letter Φ. This helps explain why Φ never goes alone. It always accompanies signifier one. About which one cannot say, about which in a fundamental way is unsayable, one cannot give it a complete consistency in body. It must be left to embody, in forms of metaphor (subjects of knots) and signifying ideas that come to it as a living name. It is not a matter of saying that because you are a man, you cannot have a feminine jouissance or that because you are a woman, you have no phallic value. In a fundamental way, *there is one sex* is a hypothesis on the existence of a subjective position irreducible to conditions of object choice.

Let us posit that for the psychoanalyst, Φ is like an infinite; as an infinite, it is missing and never full. This means that it is not desire in itself, though it supports a subject in situating subjective positions. The point to emphasize is that it can only function as a signifier of a difference of modalities.[7] This is a point of invariance.

Notes

1 This is close to Aristotle's logic especially as he develops it with regard to how the shape of the letter exists in effect of its movements (Books I and X of *Metaphysics*).

2 Sigmund Freud, "The Infantile Genital Organization (An Interpolation into the Theory of Sexuality)," in *The Ego and the Id and Other Works: 1923–1925*, ed. and trans. James Strachey, The Standard Edition of the Complete Psychological Works of Sigmund Freud, vol. 19 (London: Vintage, 2001 [1923]), 139–46; Sigmund Freud, "Femininity," in *New Introductory Lectures on Psychoanalysis and Other Works: 1932–1936*, ed. and trans. James Strachey, The Standard Edition of the Complete Psychological Works of Sigmund Freud, vol. 22 (London: Vintage, 2001 [1933]), 112–35.

3 'I have still on no account said what this phallus is' (Lacan, *Or Worse . . .*, 35).

4 In the seminar on *The Four Fundamental Concepts of Psychoanalysis*, Lacan shows how the Other functions as gaze. Lacan, *The Four Fundamental Concepts of Psychoanalysis*.

5 Lacan presents this in the session titled 'A Love Letter' in *Encore*. I prefer to call it a matheme. Lacan, *On Feminine Sexuality: The Limits of Love and Knowledge*.

6 This is relevant from the fact that regions of incest exist in 'a man' and in 'a woman', and such regions exist no more or less in one than in the other.

7 It is very near to the mathematical concept of a differential.

Chapter 7

Psychoanalytical invariance

Starting from this, the invariance of Φ means that 'woman' and 'man' are not categories of sex. There is no difference between sexes or genders that we can produce from an attribution of being or explain by a quality. Φ is a way of characterizing 'a woman' or 'a man' by a question of substance. It is necessary to give up the idea that psychoanalysis studies the social roles and sexual practices of individuals. This allows us to go much deeper into what is at play in the linkage between sex and nomination without resorting to ideological or cultural productions—productions of the universal that cannot be established with any consistency in the clinic. What, then, can we say about 'man'/'woman'?

This is difficult because sexuation implies that we start from lack as something that exists but cannot be represented. This is quite apart from philosophies of sex and gender that start from representations of lack. It is also counterintuitive to the common uses of words and grammar. This obliges us to continue developing what is meant by the phallus. What psychoanalysis calls the phallus has no possible content; in itself, it has no referentiality or representation. Philosophies of sex and gender interpret the phallus as to content. They think that the phallus has a content in the sense that the difference between sexes is consistent.[1] The clinic teaches us that the phallus is not the thing. One can no more say what the phallus is than one can picture empty space. It is impossible to deduce any sexual code from it. This impossibility implies an *invariance*: *there is one sex*. This invariance is written under the form of Φ. Φ is a point of real in every subject that is realized by each subject in a singular manner.

Let us posit that the letter Φ indicates covariation for two neighboring events: the passage of the signifier to jouissance and the extensions of jouissance into (R, S, I).[2] It is crucial here to grasp Φ is *a psychoanalytic letter*; it is not a symbol. By letter, I am trying to take into account the function of the return of repression. It is an effect of speech. A letter helps give a place to something that has no imaginary and cannot be fantasized. This is why the signifier 'man' or the signifier 'woman' is not so much an identificatory mark as a letter extracted from the body, which as lack, generates desire.

In philosophical approaches, we see the idea that invariance is an attribution of being to sex.[3] This follows from the supposition that the phallus has a content and

DOI: 10.4324/9781003366096-7

that it is the male organ par excellence. Such a supposed equivalence forms the conditions that the individual is obliged to follow in order to be a subject having an objective value.[4] The assumption of such an equivalence makes immediate socio-political sense. Feminist philosophy asks us to distinguish among social sex, biological sex, and cultural sex. For practical reasons pertaining to our socio-political realities, it is necessary to make these distinctions. Doing so helps us see that in following the path of religion, we obtain precritical concepts of nature, which insist that there is nothing for us to change.

Following the path of gender theory, we no longer say 'woman' or 'man.' We say something about gender in the sense that roles are reconducted through discourses of power. This is partially true.[5] Gender theory makes important advances in saying that gender does not define who you are. In the same instant, it looks to culture and politics to define gender on the basis of thinking that gender is a causality of the social and the political. In this search, gender theory reduces nomination to a cultural condition that pertains to external norms and conducts of reality. Psychoanalytic experience teaches us something else. Nomination is a necessary privation of the other sex, which is marked with an irreducible difference in jouissance.

It is indeed true that we imagine the phallus in the male organ. Psychoanalytic experience also shows that this happens. There is an implication that we are obliged to take account of: the repression of the jouissance of the body by phallic jouissance is tied to the emergence of the speaking subject. Such a link is imagined as a loss of the mother/child jouissance. Here, jouissance becomes a jouissance of sense, which is imagined as an organ in eroticism. In effect, the real of jouissance of the body is put at a distance by the jouissance induced by passing into language.

In the case of Little Hans, we see this with the deployments of the signifier *widdler*. The confrontation with the lack of the penis on the body of the mother as a structure is something the subject cannot avoid to think. *Thinking it* gives the concept of the phallus an imaginary consistency. This helps explain why, for little Hans, the penis will become the unary trait.

We come to what psychoanalysis calls the *phallus*. It is very difficult to perceive and accept that the phallus is empty of all possible content. It has no representation in itself. It is nothing else but a knowledge with no definition. Because one can no more say it than picture a space without a hole, it is also what ensures that there must be something repressed in order to suppose that there is an empty space where there may be meaning and signification. In effect, it compels a subject to make a difference, but it has no presence of difference. What is called the symbolic phallus emerges out of this fundamental lack as a substitutive horizon to it and to the privation continuously transmitted through nomination. The signifier Φ is an equivalent to the satisfaction, which, also in a fundamental way, is missing. In effect, Φ is a statement. For example, in saying *une* or *un* in French, we rediscover the phallus as ambivalent and ambiguous. As such, S_1 also refers to the symbolic phallus as something that appears to the subject like a trinodal call to metaphorize names-of-the-father through spaces separated by letters. Φ is a principle of differentiation that neither unveils nor hides but supports a meaning of language and in this way, generates sense.

I associate to Φ the principle of the name/names-of-the-father. I propose to call names-of-the-father *signifiers of high value*. They cannot be separated from the *law that names* as inseparable from the movement of a plurality of singular signifiers. Such a movement gives consistency to the ways we represent the subject we are from within a tridimensionality. It implies that the law that names is a result of the fundamental lack of jouissance inherent to speech. The differentiated names that the subject can realize are inseparable from the movement of jouissance.

Notes

1 On this point, it is interesting to consider Judith Butler's concept of the lesbian phallus in part one of *Bodies That Matter* and Joan Copjec's interpretation of Lacan's matheme of sexuation in chapter seven of *Read My Desire*. Judith Butler, *Bodies That Matter: On the Discursive Limits of "Sex"* (New York: Routledge, 2011); Joan Copjec, *Read My Desire: Lacan against the Historicists* (Cambridge: MIT Press, 2015).
2 Extensions imply changes in position of the S_1 and S_2 in the rotations of the discourses.
3 This is shown in Butler's critique of the second sex in Simone de Beauvoir's work in her article "Sex and Gender in Simone de Beauvoir's Second Sex." Invariance is a concept borrowed from topology. It is not an idea indicating the overdetermination of the subject. Judith Butler, "Sex and Gender in Simone de Beauvoir's Second Sex," *Yale French Studies*, no. 72 (1986): 35–49.
4 That is, especially a political subject. This helps explains why some philosophers state that woman is neither one nor two or that lesbians are not women. For instance, Monique Wittig's deduction, 'lesbians are not women', supposes that 'a lesbian has to be something else, a not-woman, a not-man, a product of society, not a product of nature, for there is no nature in society' (13). Luce Irigaray, *This Sex Which is Not One*, trans. Catherine Porter (Ithaca: Cornell University Press, 1985); Monique Wittig, *The Straight Mind and Other Essays*, trans. Marlene Wildeman (Boston: Beacon Press, 1992).
5 This is partially true psychoanalytically. Where psychoanalysis makes a distinction is with respect to the Other. The Other is a subjective power; it does not designate an objective genitive.

Chapter 8

Some preliminary remarks regarding nomination

My choice to continue using terms that have a common reference follows psychoanalytic discourse. We are concerned with the question of the unconscious situation of a subject *woven* in its jouissances.[1] Psychoanalytic experience obliges us to admit starting points that are epistemologically irreconcilable with those taken by sociological or philosophical approaches to sex and gender as socio-cultural objects.[2] Such relations concerning these objects are not necessary *a priori*. For our purpose, it is necessary to admit that there is no empirical term in sex.

It is also necessary to emphasize that the psychoanalytic encounter compels us to take seriously how a subject comes to construct a perception of their singularity around a fantasy of body. By this, I mean something that is simple to state but difficult to grasp: we are compelled to accompany the subject in the ways she is obliged to construct a fantasy in order to cope with the lost/repressed jouissance. This jouissance is fundamentally missing. We are accustomed to thinking about the trials that children endure from the point of view of adults. We attribute to the child a knowledge of sex and gender. Nomination helps us highlight the extreme difficulty in defining, from within the subjectivity of each one, what may be called sexual difference. Nomination implies a transmission of structure that exists to the subject as a knowledge without definition, like a space without a hole.

Because of this, the sex of the subject is relatively undetermined. Our starting point is that of privation; one defines something by a privation of what the subject is not. This is what Aristotle found with respect to the relation between substance and statement.[3] One notices that not all the signifiers can be said at once. The subject is defined not by a quality but by *a substance*—that is, by a privation of what the subject is not. This brings us close to one of the meanings of the Oedipus complex, which is that the subject is already marked. These marks will come to function as the most important factors in Freud's infantile sexuality.[4]

In his essay 'A Child is being Beaten', Freud elucidates how the subject is realized in the continuous iteration of passage from lack to fantasy from within a structure, on the basis of a formally undecidable. He cannot say what the knowledge is made of, only that there is a statement of the subject.[5] This bears mentioning because regarding how a subject comes to be articulated in their common relations to jouissance, there remains an insuperable gap. There remains, in these relations,

DOI: 10.4324/9781003366096-8

26 Some preliminary remarks regarding nomination

an indeterminate fundamental to the statements of the subject. Psychoanalytically speaking, this implies that one cannot both say all the signifiers and put all the jouissance into the structure. There is a difference between constructing a fantasy, which is linked to a movement of a signifying network, and putting into place a fantasy, which has to do with the moment the subject confronts the obligation to resituate jouissance once a signifier has left the signifying chain. This helps clarify that the necessity to close the sentence is a consequence of the fact that transmission does not go without implying a lack in law. Indeed, as Freud found, he cannot put a consistency to the difference between the sex of the child generating the fantasy and the sex of the child being beaten.

This brings us to a question of how the one (the one child being beaten) is passing to a plurality (there are multiple children immediately unknown to the child participating in the scene of being beaten) in a fantasy. It seems then that there is not only a question of an obligation to construct a fantasy but also a question of how the putting into place a fantasy does not go without passing it to an other through alterations and elaborations. Let us distinguish that the fantasy is modalizing itself through three inseparable processes. I am trying to explain how what Freud called identification is an unceasing movement of signifiers generating jouissance and letters. For now, I will call these processes constructing a fantasy, passing in a fantasy, and putting into place a fantasy. These three are relevant from the generation of spaces where 'being beaten' is metaphorizing the incestuous love for the mother and for the father on the basis of phallic jouissance—as permitted and as forbidden. The emergence of a fantasy as a structure satisfies the experiences of deprivations of love (frustrations) while soothing the guilt associated with the affirmation of an incestuous attachment to the love of the father. In order to have the love of the parental Other, the fantasy must transform to a masochistic jouissance. We start to see the way that the principle of repression turns on a principle of transformation in which the passage of signifier to jouissance is struck by an impossibility to resituate all the jouissance.

What this means may be expressed as follows: the masochistic jouissance is not the content of the fantasy. We are confronted to a problematic concerning how the organization of a fantasy into a reality is connected to its imaginary consistency and to an iterative dynamic of conscious/unconscious thinking in the imaginary. The difficulty here is to grasp that the emergence of the existence of the fantasy is marked by an irreducibility in the imaginary dimension. When Freud notices that the signifier 'a child is being beaten' points to a problematic in regard to the little girl, he gets ahold of an inseparability between nomination and the necessity of a formal renunciation, which takes the form of 'the other sex'. It is fundamentally different to a notion of the opposite sex. A difference between sexes seems to appear as a result of the subject substituting herself for the fantasized one supposed to child and her parents. This renunciation indicates that one cannot reduce the imaginary imaginarily. An irreducibility in the imaginary dimension exists. I associate this irreducibility in the imaginary to what Lacan called lack-in-being. It is written: $-\varphi$. Here, the contributions of what Winnicott called 'the transitional object' are registered. The difference between 'boy' and 'girl' makes no fundamental difference as to the way a subject grasps the unity experienced as a fusion with the body with the maternal Other. The subject is compelled to incorporate sex by a fantasy that lacks.

We come back to the fact that the law of the prohibition of incest consists in the necessity to conceive of the symbolic as a hole in knowledge. Subjective topology helps us further grasp that this will come to help the subject in the sense that it becomes sufficiently possible to detach from imaginary elements and attach to symbolic elements. This substitutive horizon as a possible internal to the subject will come to have a deeply important function for the subject. It comes with realizing the subjective function of separation, opening the way for a differential in a fantasy.

Notes

1 I prefer to say 'woven' since this term comes from subjective topology.
2 To put it a bit differently, the psychoanalyst is concerned with the substantial existence of the subject and not the being of life. It is true that psychoanalytical work touches upon the life of persons, but the way that psychoanalysis works to construct unknown and known knowledge in the subjectivity of each one compels us to focus on hypotheses of existence, not upon questions of being (as was first thought).
3 Aristotle, "Metaphysics," 1551–728.
4 This is very near Aristotle's deduction: 'A name, e.g. "circle", means vaguely a sort of whole: its definition analyses this into particulars. Similarly, a child begins by calling all men father and all women mother, but later on distinguishes them' (*Physics*, 315).
5 'I know nothing more about it: "a child is being beaten"' (181). Sigmund Freud, "'A Child Is Being Beaten' A Contribution to the Study of the Origin of Sexual Perversions," in *An Infantile Neurosis and Other Works: 1917–1919*, ed. and trans. James Strachey, The Standard Edition of the Complete Psychological Works of Sigmund Freud, vol. 17 (London: Vintage, 2001 [1919]), 175–204.

Chapter 9

Maternal investment

We start off from the fact that a child is named 'girl' or 'boy' by the mother. This is what Freud called *a forced choice*. The moment the child is called 'boy' or 'girl' by the mother, there is an immediate renunciation. This renunciation implies a primary privation of jouissance that takes the form of the other sex. For 'boy', it is a jouissance linked to 'girl', and for 'girl', it is a jouissance linked to 'boy'. This 'other sex' will take the form of a forbidden jouissance.

The mother names the child 'girl' or 'boy' more or less in accordance with reality. By reality, we are not referring to an empirical, social reality. I mean something close to what Freud called the *reality principle*. In fact, it is not easy to give a concrete psychoanalytic definition of reality. We can say that the real of the subject is not the social reality of the world. Lacan helped specify this definition by making a distinction between structure and S_1.[1] There is no signifier that does not go with an effect of inducing a real inherent to the structure. We see reality through a fantasy; it is in effect of introducing a referent in the effort to overcome or avoid what is experienced as fundamentally missing and without equivalence.

When the mother calls the child 'a boy' or 'a girl', she is naming a subject that comes to exist in the structure. This means that the child is immediately deprived of a part he or she has not. For a moment, the child is situated in the place of the mother's object (a) and is thus a part of her fantasy. We call this *a maternal investment*. The investment is a necessary condition of nomination in the sense that it supports the transmission of the structure as the law of castration. The first nomination involves a transmission of a fantasy that the child is compelled to construct. Nomination comes with a knowledge of a sexual code. This is one of the meanings of the Oedipus complex.

Because such a transmission also does not involve an equivalence of desire, the child is obliged to construct it by fantasizing this link on the basis of what she will think and perceive as her Other's demands. This is why fantasy refers to the finding of objects; it is not in itself the object.[2] One has to recognize that, at a certain point, it is impossible to reproduce another's subjectivity. This is why I emphasize that the child is pushed to find a place in the structure and to designate herself there as a subject. The child is compelled to make a difference in the sense that she must generate from within her own double structure of lack, a space different to a perceived

DOI: 10.4324/9781003366096-9

imaginary and a space differentiated from the other's signifiers. To this 'make a difference', I associate the activity of constructing one's own knot. The following figure expresses a maternal investment:

It is important here to perceive that the mother transmits, through the continuous flow of speech, a structure in the sense of an incompleteness and inconsistency. The symbolic phallus, S_1, and the real are always present in the transmission of the speech of the Other. The speech of the mother is like an infinite from which the child will extract what will come to constitute his or her own unconscious arrangement of signifiers.

Notes

1 Lacan, *Or Worse* . . . .
2 This is why it is impossible to know all possible variations. It is also in this sense that we may say that there are infinite scenarios.

Chapter 10

Symbolic nomination and redoubling

Let us posit that nomination is fundamentally *an unconscious symbolic nomination*. Here, it is crucial to distinguish that this is a nomination to the symbolic. It is essentially a process of privation that includes two things: a mark in jouissance and a signifier. As such, it is a point of real for every subject, in every subjectivity. What this means may be expressed as follows: nomination has only two major modalities of lack: a lack in the imaginary and a lack in the symbolic. In this sense, it is beyond any image of a mother or woman. Although nomination comes from a situation of lack in the woman, it does not come from a point of envy or from the ego. The mother nominates her child from her own situation of lack in order to have the desire of the child. As psychoanalytic experience shows, a 'woman' concerns a lack in the signifier and a lack in the organ. However, it is a mistake to think that the organ is the biological organ. What psychoanalysis calls 'organ' is a metaphor in the imaginary. The organ is situated in the real of the imaginary dimension and is linked to an irreducibility of the $-\varphi$ (lack-in-being). The organ is an object helping to give a situation to the difference between 'woman'/'man' on the basis of not being able to conceptualize it otherwise.

'A woman' has some relation to the external world and to what is familiar in the common usage of the word. From the point of view of psychoanalysis, it is an error to think that woman is linked to a physical body or a historical object. It has to do with how modalities of the signifier Φ are situated in the imaginary and in the symbolic, and as a result, always go along with something else.

One of the reasons it is necessary to keep the reference to the mother is because for the subject, it has an equivalence to being. This helps us state another hypothesis. The structure is transmitted as a hole in the sense of an incompleteness and an inconsistency. Because of this, the subject cannot avoid conceptualizing the body as a hole through which the subject must pass in order to have the desire of the other or fulfill the missing jouissance felt as lacking in the body. Psychoanalysis conceptualizes this with the term 'autoerotic'. Although there are plenty of justifiable reasons for studying the functions of autoeroticism in subjectivity, it seems to me that this can result in too much of an emphasis on, for example, the role of the mother and that of a passing to the object.[1]

DOI: 10.4324/9781003366096-10

I am here making a distinction between autoeroticism and *redoubling of nomination* to help explain how the separation between subjective position and object choice is appearing and working for the subject. Although they are implicated in the other, they are not one in the same. Autoeroticism refers to elements stuck in the imaginary. Redoubling of nomination implies a partial *detachment* of imaginary elements and the *attachment* to symbolic elements of the unconscious. This allows us to grasp that from within the continuous speech of the mother, the signifiers of high value are continuously extracted by the subject on the basis of what are thought as objects of the demand/desire of the Other. When we place too much of an emphasis on the mother's desire or the desire of the father, we miss the fact that what remains for the subject is an obligation to name himself or herself as a subject from within a double signifying structure. This is what I call *redoubling of nomination*.

For example, in the case of the Wolf Man, the signifier груша is an autonomination of the subject, a way of saying: I am your little one, a piece of your flesh. Without saying it, груша is the way he designates himself as the child of this mother and that father. In going towards the supposed object of the mother's desire, the signifier груша passes to an element of the jouissance supposed to the father. In effect, груша cancels the mother's desire in favor of succeeding to a position near the father. In this sense, the Wolf Man beats out mother's place in order to name his position as the one loved by the father. Coextensive to this passage of the signifier, the jouissance induced by груша instantiates a lost jouissance with the mother. Such an evocation gives an idea of an imaginary fusion with the mother felt like a unity of body.

We can therefore add for the Wolf Man, груша is also an instantiation of *a letter* detached of body. This removal generates a materialization of his object. I associate this removal to a subjective causality of the law. By this, I mean an emptying of a place around which a fantasy can flourish, allowing for the possibility of a subjective function of the subject that takes form as a causality. In this way, the child retains something like an independent set of reasons for his existence as having a value for others. The child builds a fantasy around the body as two separated ones (that of his 'own' body and that of the body of the parental Other).[2]

This helps us grasp that nomination has to do with a principle of obligation to separate jouissance from the law. Jouissance is always differentiating itself from the law through separation, within a continuum that is establishing a differential. Because this continuum consists of the received language transmitted through speech (as such, it is lacking), the subject must separate the first signifiers through a process of extraction in order to constitute her or his subjectivity. Here, we find the importance of the function of fantasy as not only helping to give a reason for the child's continued efforts at a separated existence. It also makes it possible for the subject to conceptualize the existence of the Other as a separated being. Fantasy helps metaphorize the *law that names as a law of transformation*. When a signifier passes to an element of jouissance, something else comes that may be described as jouissance effects. Said effects actively compel the subject to resituate the jouissance that remains as a result of the jouissance felt as missing. In reply, the subject has to nominate himself or herself once more from within a signifying structure. This nomination, which takes form as a call to resituate jouissance, is inseparable from an extraction of signifiers.

It seems that fantasy is a sign of the importance of the symbolic function of nomination. This helps explain a clinical phenomenon. In neurosis, the subject speaks as if she owns her body. In psychosis, the subject knows she does not own her body. This compels us to take deeper account of the fact that—in the space of a body, especially of one that does not belong to us—it seems that conceptualizations of 'woman'/'man' represent for everyone, in every subjectivity, an oddity in our contemporary moment.

It is important to state that the agent of nomination is variable, an x. It is inseparably linked to the signifier as a carrier of jouissance in act and in potential and to the passage of a jouissance as having an effect of a consistency, enabling the subject to speak of body. We may therefore abandon the assumption that nomination can make any sort of postulate of a universal about parental roles or about the meanings and significations 'boy' or 'girl' will come to have for a subject.

When the child passes into language, she is confronted to a lack that is experienced as awful and mortal. Correlatively, it is experienced as the possibility of overcoming it. Such an experience is correspondingly linked to the idea that there is a satisfaction—that there is something which is not lacking, and as such, is fulfilling. What suddenly appears is the possibility of a satisfaction (even if it is a feeling of a lack) that the child thinks will overcome the lack. In this moment, the child puts an equivalence to the lack as an existence in the effort to avoid or overcome it. Φ is this equivalence. In this way, it is a simple statement of the subject.

Maternal nomination is effectively something spoken of in two ways through the speech of the mother—as potential and as actual. I associate this to S_1.[3] The child knows that she is spoken by her maternal Other but cannot put any content to it. In this sense, the child receives the nomination as an appeal to situate herself in the dimension that is evoked by the call of the speech of the mother in order to give existence to that which has no concrete being or representation in itself. The child must name herself there as a subject in order to add a dimension to subjectivity that is felt as missing or lost.

To try to subjectivize this fundamental lack, the child is obliged to pass into language by speaking. But by speaking, the signifier is lacking. This tells us that speech is constrained by a lack in language and by a recognition of the lack as something fundamentally missing. There are three factors difficult to grasp and to perceive. One concerns the function of the voice as a discreet element. The child uses her voice in an effort to find a completeness to the image. It is a transmission element supporting the passage between speech and language, between language and speech as a continuum. Because such a continuum exists only by the ways a subject passes from one to the other (and moves relatively to it), we find two other factors. Language is equivalent to the perception of the body as a totality. It is linked to the presence of a law that names in its absence. The other factor concerns the fact that speech is not equivalent to the loss of the presence of the mother.

The moment the child passes into a knot of language, the maternal discourse creates in herself a lack. For example, the child needs a cuddle, and the mother is not there. The child experiences this lack as something unbearable and is compelled to call for the mother. The child notices that there is a difference between words and the real. Words are not the real of the cuddle. In a fundamental way, the real is unreachable and is felt in the experience of something missing without being to say it otherwise. As a result, there is a necessity to metaphorize the passage itself as a continuum that is otherwise missing.

Notes

1 We see this with some post-Freudians.
2 Freud tried to conceive of this point in his explanation of the linkage of the grusha scene to the initials of his name.
3 In his essay "The Unconscious" (1915) and later, in "The Ego and the Id" (1923), Freud defines a sort of 'first identification'. He describes it as a root of the superego and links this identification to the glorified figure of the father. From this, we grasp that the first identification refers to the *symbolic phallus*. Sigmund Freud, "The Unconscious," in *On the History of the Psychoanalytic Movement, Papers on Metapsychology and Other Works: 1914–1916*, ed. and trans. James Strachey, The Standard Edition of the Complete Psychological Works of Sigmund Freud, vol. 14 (London: Vintage, 2001 [1915]), 159–214. Freud, "The Ego and the Id."

Chapter 11

The link between speech and nomination

About what does psychoanalysis speak? Psychoanalysis speaks of sexuality *in excess*. This is what Freud called *infantile sexuality*. It is an utmost point of subjectivity that is neither relevant from nor derived from the life of the individual. Infantile sexuality does not speak of deviances, pathologies, or any conducts in empirical realities. This is what Lacan called *jouissance*. In a fundamental way, the object of psychoanalysis is impossible to subjectivize outside the psychoanalytical field. This is why psychoanalysis cannot produce any objectivism. Infantile sexuality is an element of repression and thus cannot be explained by any rationality. It is also why it must be admitted that the psychoanalytic object is incommensurable with physical things or philosophical entities.

In Freud's epistemology, the thing (*das Ding*) is something linked to the first move of incest as forbidden from the child to the mother. It is a remainder that is always there, compelling the subject as a remnant of her interpretation of the desires and demands of her Other. He will then try to schematize the topos of the sexual. In his *Introductory Lectures on Psychoanalysis*, Freud tries to show that *the sexual* only has its origins in the lack of jouissance of each subject. Lacan then picks up on the fact that the subject identifies infantile sexuality with the demand/ desire of the Other in its persistence. He goes further, showing that such an identification is always accompanied by the reply that the subject gives to the Other, in the ways she offers herself as an object through fantasy objects.[1]

What Freud called infantile sexuality and what Lacan calls object (a) is only what differs irreducibly from the signifier inasmuch as *it is what has not passed to the signifier by way of nomination and the speech of the maternal Other*. In a strange way, 'woman'/'man' signifiers are not spoken by the Other. As a result, infantile sexuality is something that is unknown but which does not cease calling the subject to a place. This is what I call *a knot*. It is only that which compels a subject to formations of the unconscious—to a knotting of the real, symbolic, and imaginary. From the nomination, there remains something that is like an affectation for a hole.

Starting from nomination in the symbolic, we know that it is not a sociological call to adapt to a biological or sociological construction. The subject knows (without understanding) that she is spoken by the Other. Because she cannot only

DOI: 10.4324/9781003366096-11

The link between speech and nomination **35**

be the object of the Other, she is compelled to be a subject. What is meant here by 'compelled to be a subject'? It means to have a value that calls for signification and meaning.

For example, in the case of Little Hans, there are moments in which he is compelled to perceive a -φ. Its *ek-sistence* is unbearable, and this suffering (which Freud called trauma), obliges him to extract and put the signifier *widdler* as an equivalence to it. This process is not only to do with the fact that he is confronted to the body of the mother as lacking a penis. It is also relevant from the fact that this confrontation immediately implies the impossibility to experience the mother's jouissance. The difference between the organ and the symbolic phallus appears to him, inducing the appearance of the symbolic dimension of the phallus. The status of the knowledge changes in effect of where it is situated.

The symbolic dimension of the phallus is a dimension that calls for signification with a symbolic value beyond any unconscious image of narcissism. In this sense, it is a spatiality different to the imaginary. He *knows* that the symbolic phallus exists—that something like a cuddle of language exists—*and* that he cannot put any concrete being to represent it. It is very difficult for him to be without the part he has not. In an effort to find and put an equivalence to it, one that would function to satisfy the jouissance perceived as lost/missing by bypassing it, Little Hans is forced to perceive an image that is lacking. This opens unto the possibility of putting a name to it, that is, of adding a dimension to subjectivity.

For Little Hans, *widdler* is a signifier of high value. It is a point of real where the overlapping of speech and body is designating the effect of symbolic and imaginary values necessary to jouissance. The point to emphasize is that *widdler* is an instance of a redoubling of nomination. In a certain way, it helps him get ahold of a maternal Other as something that cannot be reached and as something that exists as an infinite potentiality.

Now, we can add something to the linkage between sex and nomination. It is an iterative movement characterized by a move of the child to the mother and by a transmission of signifiers of high value to the child through the speech of the mother. The subject knows (without understanding) that he is spoken by the Other. Because he cannot only be the object of the Other, he is compelled to have a symbolic value beyond any imaginary. This is linked to the imperative that one must have a value. Access to such a value is what psychoanalysis calls phallic jouissance.

This knowledge cannot be separated from the fact that the structure is always there and that the emergence of the existence of structure is marked. It has to do with the fact that a subject is marked in their substance by a lack in jouissance and a mark in signifier. The subject finds the structure, but it is always lacking. In consequence of this, subjects are marked 'woman'/'man' by an alterity emerging in relation to deprivations in the real, the symbolic, and the imaginary (R, S, I). Here, Lacan's formula, 'there is no sexual relation', resonates. This lack immediately takes the form of the other sex, which is also lacking—now in the form of dimensions missing in the subject's subjective position. In this way, *widdler* is also expressing closures of space by designating spaces of appearance where there are no common elements between an intimate point and a point external to the subject.

Little Hans helps us grasp the fact that the law is experienced as an imperative to have a value. This is a point of real he cannot avoid to think. In going towards individual animals, the body of his mother, his father's body, and so forth, *widdler* turns following a question: *why*? This is linked to the presence of the law, which always seems to appear in the difference of two. The signifier *widdler* expresses the ways the reply of the subject is in jouissance.

Note

1 Jacques Lacan, *Formations of the Unconscious*, ed. Jacques-Alain Miller, trans. Russell Grigg, The Seminar of Jacques Lacan, Book V (Malden: Polity, 2017).

Chapter 12

The difficulty of interpretation

One of the deeper obscurities in psychoanalysis is that infantile sexuality cannot be formulated in terms of rationality, but its interpretation through metaphor is necessary. It also implies that it is a kind of rationality that goes into the structure. In a certain way, it is tied to subjective effects called meaning and signification, which are unceasingly generated by interpretations of the unconscious. Such interpretations are themselves tied to existential positions of each subject in their links to intimate faults.[1] Infantile sexuality is woven of an obligation to speak about something that has no being but which has real effects. This is why it is not a thing in itself or an entity.

To speak about the real is a kind of methodology. We cannot avoid the fact that the real has only to do with existence differentiated from being. It is linked to the ways every subject is marked and how those marks are metaphorizing jouissance in a fantasy. Subjective topology is a way of characterizing the irreducible singularity in every subjectivity, in every knotting. There are indefinitely many knots. I can formulate the singularity of a knotting in this way: it is where the topos of the subject is and where the subject finds the words to help manifest it.

It seems to me that Poincaré grasped something of a psychoanalytical truth. What he called changes in position are linked to the fact that among all the changes we can perceive in a body, those that are cancelled by a movement are those marked by their simplicity.[2] We obtain a form of *infinitely close* that we call a neighborhood. What Lacan called *point at infinity*, Φ, also describes the non-existence of the *infinite straight line*.[3] There is no father that orders all the jouissance.

What comes to matter for a subject in the experience of a psychoanalytical cure is the process of extraction of an infinite of series signifiers and objects that allow the subject to perceive in a deeper way, where they are in their fantasy. It is necessary here to state that these spatial operations are characterized by an unceasing movement from finite to infinite, from infinite to finite. This movement, which we call a psychoanalytical operation, is one of the infinites that Freud found. He found that the way the unconscious exists is as an infinite, but that as an infinite, it is missing. It never stops iterating itself as different to itself. Structure is a reply to a lack in signifier and a mark in jouissance. It is a result of what is missing in the subject as jouissance. From this, we obtain a definition of jouissance as a compact space relevant from the ways the subject extracts and puts signifiers near gaps in words.[4]

DOI: 10.4324/9781003366096-12

38 The difficulty of interpretation

In a certain way, what psychoanalysis calls truth is linked to the ways a subject can access or cannot what for them alone are their unknown, enigmatic points. To try to interpret them by the letters that help metaphorize traces of jouissance is very difficult because it implies a radical incompleteness characterizing any theory and the impossibility of knowledge as cumulative or totalizable. We say truth is an invention of knowledge because it is only a question of getting ahold of the signifiers that matter for the subject and that in a real way, open the possibility for perceiving how the existential positions situating a subject are tied to unconscious jouissance and desire.

Let us return to the speech of the mother. This speech exists to the subject like an infinite. I associate to this infinite the incestuous demand of the Other, which calls for fusion and reunification. In reply, the child is always extracting signifiers in an effort to get back what has been irretrievably lost and which is experienced as missing. These extractions are always producing a feeling of lack in the existential positions $(-\varphi)$. The functions of φ (always partialized) are in every moment of subjectivity and in every theory. It is necessary to grasp that one of the effects of Φ as a point of real from which the subject is expelled is an immediate transformation of an infinite that is missing into a twisting point.[5] It seems that this transformation of Φ, which henceforth becomes a real, supports the supposition that there exists such a thing as an absolute, unlimited jouissance and that it is something that can be possessed by only one. Starting from this, the subject can make a series of statements regarding what is true or false in relation to the law. The subject can think that there exists one for whom the phallic function does not work and who is thus above the law.

There is still a question of the infinite straight line as relevant from a formal renunciation. It is this problematic that I am also trying to explain. Shifting the emphasis to the law of the unconscious brings us closer. There remains *a wish* for the law to guarantee that we shall not meet with any contradiction after some set of assertions. This 'some' may be a number as large as one pleases. But it must be finite, that is, limited. Why? In order to have the right to lay down a system of postulates, we require assurance that somewhere, they are not contradictory. The treatise of the *a priori* is written with the object of overcoming the difficulties raised by this wish. The wish is manifestly assured in interests in contradictions and antimonies, from which the belief that it is possible to construct a science of *all* is born. We may remove the problematic from our view, but it does not resolve the fact that we meet it in the efforts of logic.

When Freud realizes the fact that penis envy transforms into a wish for a child, he perceived in a much deeper way that the real fundamental to every subject is the jouissance of the maternal body. This transformation is a question of how a subject is singularizing itself through a fantasy, while relieving itself of having a pretension to a universal.[6] It is something fundamentally to do with a moment characterizing the substance of the subject as at once an out-of-sense and beyond any imaginary of object. In effect, the subject is split between signifier and presence. In other words, Freud grasped that the word is not the thing, and was able to put a methodology to

The difficulty of interpretation 39

the question of how this non-existent jouissance is working and appearing for the subject.

I associate the non-existence of the jouissance of the maternal body to the infinite line extending to infinity. There is no way to experience it or have any knowledge of it. There is no actual existence of it. It is non-existent and ungraspable except by a formal rejection. It remains important that the subject has recourse to hallucinate this non-existent, limitless horizon. This imaginary will extend into the illusory that characterizes the Other's jouissance. This renunciation of the primary privation coming from nomination will take form as the other sex, as permitted or as forbidden. This allows us to see that that the existential positions of the subject are separated from object choice in impassable ways.

It seems to me that Winnicott clearly recognized a truth when he said that the transitional object exists only as a passage—in act and in potential—between nothing and a something (between castration and jouissance). It is only something that is realized as a relation of a subject to another subject. What he called 'maternal phallus' is linked to the subjective effects of the grasp of the transitional object. Freud linked the object to the phallus and the organ. Now, we can say that it is only a relation to the phallus.

Indeed, the subject finds that not all language has meaning and signification. This is coextensive to the fact that by speaking, the signifier is lacking. The moment the subject goes into language by a process of extracting signifiers and objects, there is also an immediate confrontation to a disappearance of jouissance of a maternal body. The subject experiences it as unbearable. There is no jouissance that exists as a being. Because of this, the phallic function returns us to other spaces of jouissance. What psychoanalysis calls *speech* exists as *a turning*. Φ turns following a supposition of a lack. Following what Freud and Lacan discovered with respect to the phallic function, I write the function of speech with the letter Ψ. My hypothesis is that it is an invariant cycle in which the movements S_1 and S_2 are covariant with respect to the condition of Φ vanishing (unlimited jouissance vanishes). Because of this, Φ operates from within the structure as a finite at infinity. In this way, it is limited and exists in two modalities of phallic jouissance: as permitted or as forbidden. Signifiers organized in a signifying chain (language) is not jouissance.

When a signifier passes to jouissance, that is, when there is a jouissance in act, the signifying chain disappears. Immediately, there is a perception that an equivalence can be put to overcome this disappearance, which is experienced as unbearable. This perception of a supposed equivalence takes the form of a satisfaction/dissatisfaction. For example, when the child perceives a smile on the father's face and identifies herself to it. In the same moment, the identification with the smile invokes the presence of the maternal Other as lacking. The identification to the smile (here functioning as a signifier) emerges jointly as cause of the father's desire and the unity that cancels the desire of the mother.

More formally, the starting point of psychoanalytical discourse is like a point of the bifurcation of a skeleton. In itself, it is a process involving the signifying structure of speech in its coextensions with language. Such a process is supported by a

40 The difficulty of interpretation

formal cut between signifier and jouissance. This cut generates a neighborhood of a kind of double point (a mark in signifier and a lack in jouissance) from which the subject is expelled. The two are not knotted in a signifying chain but seem to refer to how jouissance emerges jointly as an expression of the body the subject does not have and as a kind of unity of structure for which there is no concept. The difficulty is to conceive of the status of the signifier in a hylomorphism with jouissance.[7] It carries the potentiality to be realized as jouissance. In act, such jouissance is realized as speech, which, in turn, implies a fall of the jouissance that immediately compels the subject to try to reconstitute the missing jouissance. Here, an obscurity makes itself felt. The moment there is a disappearance of jouissance, the subject feels it in an emptying of spaces, in the body, and is immediately called to resituate jouissance. It is the moment when the subject experiences a sort of collapse in the fundamental fantasy as a call to make once more a tie between signifier and jouissance. This call to 'couple' supports the subject in finding, in the perception of a body of 'the other sex', an equivalent of the lost presence of 'father' and 'mother'. This equivalence is associated with inducing forms of satisfaction and dissatisfaction. I can help summarize this process with the following formulation: the body is where the jouissance is not.

We now come to the question of how the linkage between sex and nomination is a neighboring of the real and the imaginary, implying a nomination of the symbolic. From the symbolic, there emerges something that names in being limited. As a result, the ways a subject thinks sex is linked to the body will be a question of how the lack is functioning or not to give a kind of certitude of the unity of the structure. Here 'one' is an idea of an imaginary fusion that comes from the tie of the child with the mother. The unity is the structure. If the child feels this unity, she has something that she cannot express but which is designated by an S_1. In neurosis, this S_1 also means something like a unity of the structure emerging from a feeling of existence. In this sense, an existence position is assured. The child knows that she belongs to a circle of close ones, a family.

It is important to take into account how this certitude functions for the subject. In neurosis, we observe that it never ceases to generate an image of the body as a spatiality differentiated from an ideal. Such a differential helps the subject to construct a fantasy and works as something around which a fantasy flourishes. In my experience working with psychosis, this position of the S_1 as a certitude of having an existential position linked to a feeling of a unity of structure is missing or is extremely partialized. The Other and the object (a) are not separated. The Other does not lack. As a result, the subject cannot or has extreme difficulty in experiencing herself as a having a body that belongs to her and which she owns. The contributions of Piera Aulagnier's work on the linkage between psychosis and potentiality are registered here. She shows that, in psychosis, the subject cannot name herself as this child of that mother and that father. That is, the subject has difficulty perceiving causality. I propose that this is an effect of a formal cut between signifier and jouissance that is missing to the subject. It helps explain why in psychosis, there is a continuous interpenetration of ego and id. To put it topologically, the infinite series of R, S,

I exists in a continuum with the function of the gaze as a continuity.[8] As a result, only one consistency is deployed. Let us posit that such a formal cut is what allows the subject to perceive the difference between 'woman'/'man' as a radical alternative. Both neurosis and psychosis teach us that nomination can become a cruel superego. In psychosis, it seems that the subject has no way to escape it or only has extremely partialized ways to do so.

Subjective topology helps bring forth letters as functioning to metaphorize jouissance as an experience of *a lost/loss of* source felt within the body. In the same moment, letters allow a subject to access a lack in the other sex with the help of discreet elements that are the signifiers of the subject. What Bion called 'elements' helps us specify not only that each space implies the privation of the other space and consequently, *in the form* of the other sex but also that 'by an element', we mean a push to transmit structure.[9] By transmission of structure, I am trying to describe how the separation of letters and signifiers allows for a neighboring of the symbolic phallus Φ, which is felt as a condition to have value for others. It is by an element of transmission, which is no other than *voice*, that the passage from speech to language, and from language to speech, is a differential movement of opposites. Such a movement supports subjective existence within differentiated positions. What this means may be expressed as follows: nomination also implies a passage of a fantasy to an other, obliging the subject to make a subjective separation. This is the principle of an internal finality inherent in the structure. Lacan called this principle the *knot to three*.

Henceforth, it will be a question of how a subject's jouissance is made out of letters and how signifiers transform into elements of jouissance. By proposing the real as a covariation, it is this principle of transformation of unconscious speech that I am trying to explain. The difficulty is to grasp that nomination of the symbolic is not a nomination of jouissance. This is why it is important to perceive that naming has the effect of adding a dimension to subjective existence. A name carries us to the fact that we are dealing with a system that only acts because it is made up of pure differences, that is, of unary traits borrowed in effect of the fact that the law has no essential physical characteristics. A name helps us approach the real, but it reminds us that we cannot touch it.[10] Let us recall that the way Freud named the clinical structures was not by the pathologies or the troubles but *by a reply of the subject to the feeling of lack.*[11]

Notes

1 This is how I interpret the inseparability of the variable x in relation to the places and their changing terms in Lacan's matheme for sexuation.
2 Poincaré, *Science and Method.*
3 Lacan, "Seminar XXII: RSI," 1974–75. Jacques Lacan, *The Sinthome*, ed. Jacques-Alain Miller, trans. A. R. Price, The Seminar of Jacques Lacan, Book XXIII (Cambridge: Polity, 2016).
4 In borrowing from Lacan the concept of compact space to make jouissance more precise, I am trying to explain how the movement of signifiers on the borders of the object

42 The difficulty of interpretation

(a) generates a neighboring of regions of jouissance and spaces empty of jouissance. That is, I am trying to explain how object (a) is existing as a differential of movement among letters, jouissance, and signifiers. In more concrete terms, how can an acceptance of sex transform a subject, since this is what clinical experience shows happens?

5 This twisting point corresponds to a point at infinity the moment it transforms into a notion of an infinite straight line (such as the moebian representation of the structure of the unconscious indicates). It's what Freud called the preconscious. It is linked to a moment of castration when the space (a) is no longer fulfilled by a fantasy but is a pure lack. By the notion of an infinite straight line, I mean something close to a resonance of a lack in all dimensions of speech linked to the ways the subject experiences the signifying movement by passing through sub-spaces empty of jouissance (body). Later in the essay, I try to explain this through *voice*.

6 This is also how I interpret Lacan's statement, there is no other of the other. Here, is it difficult to perceive that a singular universal is different from an abstract universal, which concerns a universe of intention and thus with meaning and reference. On this point, it is interesting to consider Jacques Derrida's critique of presence in his philosophy of arche-writing. There is the thought that the trace is a presence that supposes the existence of written traces as originary. From a psychoanalytic point of view, this misses how substance, as lacking, is outside all predication. Jacques Derrida, *Of Grammatology*, trans. Gayatri Chakravorty Spivak (Baltimore: Johns Hopkins University Press, 1998).

7 This is meant in an Aristotelian sense.

8 For example, in the case of Schreber, when he is called to a symbolic position (that of judge), he has difficulty sustaining it.

9 In *Elements of Psychoanalysis*, we see that psychoanalytical elements are invoked as an effect of a neighboring with empty spaces. Bion, *Elements of Psychoanalysis*.

10 In this way, *a name* is close to Cantor's statement: there is no actual infinity.

11 To help give a sense to what I am trying to say with regard to neighboring, I place an emphasis on '*by a*'. It is an evocation of *an infinitely close*. Because the reply of the subject is something that emerges in effect of the lack, the unconscious sayings of the subject are motivated by signifiers. The crucial factor here is that the lack is not an element in the structure. Because of this, the movements of the subject of speech generate a neighboring between a signifier showing the lack in the meaning in the Other and the appearance of the phallus in a symbolic dimension.

Chapter 13

Signifiers 'man', 'woman'

Semblant of body

We come to questions concerning what is a fantasy and what it is made of.

Transference teaches us that what exists for the subject is a certain arrangement of signifiers that appears to us as a language in which signifiers represent the subject we are for the Other. The way signifiers are arranged is in relation to the way in which, in feeling compelled to be a subject, the subject is obliged to fantasize the non-existence of the link to the Other. The subject is forced to take an object as a support. Fantasy thus takes the form of *a choice of object*. For Freud, this will come to define oedipal sexuality. In hysteria, it is linked to the way an incestuous desire is realized by passing through an unconscious love of the self in the image. Freud called this masochism. Lacan called it jouissance of the Other. It results in reducing the subject to annihilation. In this sense, it is beyond everyday sexuality; it does not pertain to the incorporation of sex or gender with biological organs or cultural patterns. It only has to do with the way the subject, by means of fantasizing an exteriority, perceives sex as missing in the unconscious image of the body and what in the signifier is lacking as jouissance.

Regarding the hysterical symptom, Freud found that repression is the principle mechanism.[1] The mechanism of repression generates two major modalities of lack (never completely separated) open to the subject as a way to realize a fundamental fantasy. There is what we can call a hysteria of conversion (Freud sometimes called this *somatic compliance*). This is the metaphor of incest in the Oedipus complex. There is also what we can call a hysteria of anxiety where the object of incest is not displaced as metonymic. As a result, unconscious anxiety consists in a defense against the perception of the Other. This is why Lacan, differently from Freud who said anxiety is without an object, emphasizes that anxiety has one. The object of incest is metonymized in anxiety.

When Freud grasped that neurotic symptoms are a result of a fantasy, he made more precise the fact that what he called the drive exists as a desire marked by a lack. One of the meanings of this is that the unconscious image (our narcissism) is always lacking. In reformulating the Freudian drive as object (a), Lacan picks up on the fact that narcissism corresponds to the emergence of the structure. It is inseparable from what Freud was trying to schematize with the help of the term *nachträglichkeit* and what Lacan calls *après-coup*. To help make a step forward, the hypothesis that the structure is occurring as a hole helps here.

DOI: 10.4324/9781003366096-13

44 Signifiers 'man', 'woman'

One of the meanings of 'deferred action' is that there is no beginning or ending to the structure. There is no moment of origin. The emergence of the existence of structure is an effect of language. The 'deferred action' of language consists in the pushing for the emergence on the structure, that is, on our substantiality. We come back to the question of the symbolic law of the unconscious. The law takes the form of sexual difference. As a result, we continue to infer a fiction of language that obliges us to continue thinking the meaning of language. This relates to the function of the logos. It is by the return of all the signifiers that language is constituted as having a capacity to make sense and to be something that is communicated to others. Following Wittgenstein's deductions from everyday language, we cannot avoid the constraint that by structure, it means that *we cannot seize it*. As he puts it: 'From it is humanly impossible to gather immediately the logic of language'.[2] One cannot say all the signifiers. Because of this, language is in what we are; and we can only define it with the help of the symbolic. Jouissance is effectively what makes the body consistent and what makes life. Starting from this, we can posit that what is lacking in the subject as jouissance (as an infinite line that extends to the infinite) finds its equivalence in a recourse to an effectiveness, that is, to *wirklichkeit* (reality). This is why reality is not the knot. The knot is the real of the subject and as such, is a support of the subject.

This helps clarify that narcissism corresponds to the way the emergence of the structure is particularized in such a way that the subject obtains something like a new structure within it. This structure is composed of two modalities. One corresponds to the cut in jouissance of the body transmitted by the speech of the maternal Other in its expressions to a lack in signifier. This implies an articulation to a tridimensionality. This is the virtual image transmitted in the maternal speech. The other consists of the two marks corresponding to the two spaces of the cut 'woman'/'man'. It is crucial here to emphasize that the two modalities of structure are relevant from an active difference between spaces of representation and structure.

We obtain an ensemble composed of a subjective image and its functioning as a mirror. This ensemble appears to form a reciprocal of the virtual image coming from the speech of the mother and a real image of the other that captivates and gives the subject support. This image of the other is a phallically invested other inasmuch as it is where the phallus appears in the imaginary and not in a symbolic form. Such a real image will come to work as the 'father' of reality. One of the reasons that our unconscious image of narcissism elude us is because it is a reply to fundamental lack on the basis of what is felt as missing in a body as a unity. It is an unceasing process of trying to get it back that takes take the form of building the mirror of the Other by tying it to the signifiers 'man'/'woman'. The subject tries to make a body of it. Such a 'mirror' will come to operate as a unary trait. In this sense, S_2 carries an ego ideal in relation to other imaginary identifications.

This helps us clarify why there are three vectors in Lacan's matheme for sexuation. The vectors refer to the way a subject is compelled to fantasize the lack in the Other in order to differentiate within it what is lacking in signifier as jouissance.

One notices that in order to speak of body, one must speak of consistence. In referring to the ways the subject fantasizes the lack in the Other, the vectors aim for the emergence of a desire. In going towards an alterity marking the perception of a body of woman ($\cancel{La}$) and the lack thought of in the man as something removed from his body, the vectors are indexed to an effort of the subject to create a desire out of nothing. In this way, the vectors are covariant with respect to the movements of prohibitions and incest in the subject's relation with the Other. They indicate a fundamental impossibility to reconstitute a missing jouissance and the fact that the principle of prohibition is transgressed by a fantasy, which is turning around a metaphor of incest.

The deferred action of language tells us that jouissance exists as a differential of the movement of signifiers. To help develop this point, I prefer the term *closure*. This helps make more precise the distinction between sexuation and sexuality. Sexuation only has to do with subjective positions of existence separated from conditions of object choice. As a speaking body, the speaking being is continuously realizing a body of speech that gives consistency to the principle of repression. What in everyday language is called sexuality is conceived of and defined in relation to the ways in which sex and gender are socio-historical objects that produce and invade ideologies. As it concerns the subject of the unconscious, sexuation is in consequence of the fact that the sex of the subject is a point of real. Because of this, the subject is obliged to pass through logical modalities of speech (the necessary, the contingent, the impossible, the possible) in order to give a situation to jouissance.

Notes

1 Sigmund Freud, "Inhibitions, Symptoms and Anxiety," in *An Autobiographical Study: Inhibitions, Symptoms and Anxiety; The Question of Lay Analysis and Other Works: 1925–1926*, trans. James Strachey, The Standard Edition of the Complete Psychological Works of Sigmund Freud, vol. 20 (London: Vintage, 2001 [1926]), 75–176.
2 Wittgenstein, *Tractatus Logico-Philosophicus*, 45.

Chapter 14

The psychoanalytical group

From subjective topology, we obtain deeper insight into the fact that one of the ways a subject obtains relief from the continued dissatisfactions, frustrations, and constraints that inhabit the social relation is to hystericize it. The discourse of the hysteric is a reply to feelings and perceptions of lack continuously generated by the social tie that, in turn, obligates each one to manage their jouissance to value and to enjoy. It is a question of a kind of export into a behavior that resembles the one we see every day when we meet a human being. It is important to recognize that in the psychoanalytical field, the social is an imperative composed of a fundamental significance of individuality and a way of including the value of the subject.

When Freud observed that the notion of impossibility is removed from the individual in a group, he got ahold of something that is complicated to perceive and articulate.[1] The psychoanalytical concept of the 'group' is often confused with the social as pertaining to the empirical realities of our world. They imply one another, but they are not the same. The question of what is meant by the psychoanalytical group is, in a fundamental way, a question of transmission of structure as a modality of generation. It is a point of real for every subject; and it is in every layer, always generating a real in every dimension of subjectivity. Nomination helps us explain that structure is transmitted in the sense of an incompleteness. This generates extremities in position that we come to call the individual and the universal. When the group corresponds to the point where the subject is commanded to a value for others, it generates a neighborhood in which the two extremities are effectively, infinitely close. A sense of an unlimited jouissance is restored to the two. A question that remains to be dealt with is this: how is the group of the fundamental modalities of generation (lack in signifier and what is missing in the subject as jouissance) linked to the structure of identification?

Psychoanalytic experience teaches us that the passage of one generation to another implies a change in the status of knowledge. It is not a question of *what is* the knowledge to be sought. Rather, it is a question of *where the knowledge is* and *in what does it consist*. In his writing of the four discourses, Lacan helped show that the discourse of the master produces a subjection to a signifier that orders all the others.[2] In this sense, the subject knows they are subjected. Interpreted as to the existential positions of each individual, one has to admit that this discourse is an

DOI: 10.4324/9781003366096-14

The psychoanalytical group   47

agent of a symbolic order. From this, it remains necessary to reduce the discourse, which is experienced as a normative power, and move to simplify it. We simplify it when we perceive that it is not possible for one signifier to give all the jouissance. Lacan makes a simple hypothesis: by a simple rotation, it turns. From this, we obtain a definition of unconscious discourse as consisting of four modalities of speech where the elements and places are moving.

This implies that the places where *a appears as* function as a semblant. In the rotations of unconscious discourse, we find speech aiming at seeming. It does not aim at being. This tells us that the semblant helps to designate interrelations between jouissance and the signifiers as expressions of the real of the subject (spaces of appearances within spaces of representation). Said semblant is no other than jouissance, as missing, which never ceases to generate knowledge effects. Knowledge effects are linked to changes in subjective position in relation to the movement of jouissance, which aims at filling empty spaces.

The discourse of the psychoanalyst helps show that an address to the divided subject opens the possibility for the subject to glimpse the repeated position occupied in a fundamental fantasy. For example, when the analysand gets ahold of the master signifiers commanding her to match the demand of the Other, there is a glimpse into the type of object she is for her Other in a fantasy. This possibility allows for the chance to interpret how S_2 as knowledge known is working for the subject to give meaning and sense to the fundamental lack carried in S_1. In this way, S_2 is a product of speech realized in the regions where the subject incorporates the demands from the Other. The discourse of the psychoanalyst supports a subject in grasping the signifiers that have functioned as lethal signifiers in the fundamental fantasy, and the fact that at certain moments, such a fantasy is always linked to the imaginary phallus and its pretensions.[3] In this way, the analyst helps the subject build a new knowledge that enables her or him to get out of an infinite of suffering.

Notes

1 '[T]he notion of impossibility disappears for the individual in a group' (77). Sigmund Freud, "Group Psychology and the Analysis of the Ego," in *Beyond the Pleasure Principle: Group Psychology and Other Works: 1920–1922*, ed. and trans. James Strachey, The Standard Edition of the Complete Psychological Works of Sigmund Freud, vol. 18 (London: Vintage, 2001), 65–144.
2 From the seminar *RSI*: 'A semblance on which there is grounded all discourse, in the first rank, the discourse of the Master which makes of the phallus the signifier index 1' (Lacan, 117).
3 This is what Freud conceptualized as the partial object of the drive.

Chapter 15

The discourse of the hysteric and jouissance

The discourse of the hysteric shows that unconscious discourse rotates following a suffering in the image. This suffering, which is the aim of the subject, is the supposition of a lack. Because of this, the supposition persists in a want of something that can soothe it or help bypass it. The spatiality of the imaginary helps us perceive that the hysteric tries to make the Other exist as a consistence by completing an unconscious image of narcissism. This is why the hysteric is one who builds her desire according to what she thinks is lacking in her Other as desire by making herself an erotic-abject object for her Other. This also helps to explain why hysteria follows a dissatisfied desire. For the hysteric, no one else can have a value but the Other. The Other is a region to which the subject is drawn by language, where it may be looked upon like a water source. It is something tied to an imaginary.

For example, in the case of Dora, the linkage between her cough and the loss of voice goes towards the cough of the father. It is a metaphor of the sexual relation with Mrs. K. For Dora, it is linked to the idea of the father's impotency. The extraction of this cough is a single trait that supports an imaginary identification with her father. Dora's cough comes to function as a unary trait, an S_2. This S_2 marks a pass to language by giving a place to the cough as something that keeps Dora fixed to the ideal father, the ego ideal. In this sense, the cough gives meaning and signification to her ideal place as a subject of exception.

In Dora's case, my hypothesis is that in her fantasy, she identifies with an image of a real woman. This identification gives her a masochistic jouissance and satisfies her guilt. It is the way she realizes saving her father from his own impotency, while overcoming him.[1] For Dora, such a fantasy is how she adds herself as an erotic-abject object (a) of her fantasy in order to complete her unconscious image of narcissism. This object is the object of a lack of jouissance. It is the dialectical object inasmuch as it never stops transforming a first lack, impossible to recover as such, in an object of fantasy. As a result, there is an incessant attempt to reconstitute the body of the Other through a fantasy in order to overcome it. Let us posit that the hysterical fantasy is constructed around the aim for the emergence of a desire between 'man' and 'woman' on the basis of a refusal to accept that the body of the Other does not exist. In Dora's case, we see that this refusal is based on a connection to Frau K's love of her father as concealing a lack in her father.[2]

DOI: 10.4324/9781003366096-15

Subjective topology helps us clarify that hysteria is characterized by a non-closure of the symbolic resulting in a partialized movement of the elements and places in the discourse of the unconscious. The master signifiers remain fixed in place, preventing the possibility of an extraction of new signifiers that would give the subject a sufficient symbolic value. In hysteria, the subject remains in an over-valuation of the narcissistic value. The partial closure of the symbolic dimension keeps the subject trapped in an infinite of an unsatisfied desire. It is effectively not closed in the sense that the subject cannot make a knotting that would reduce the suffering in an image. The following figure helps show this:

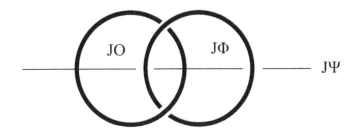

The difficulty is to perceive that this non-closure of the symbolic satisfies the way the subject remains very near the Other as a presence. In this way, the subject gives consistency to the belief that the route for attaining the love of the Other is by remaining as a surplus image that can be added/removed from the imaginary image of a union. For Dora, the body of the woman evokes such an imaginary image.

Let us now distinguish the types of jouissance within the neurotic structure. There is phallic jouissance (JΦ). I associate this to a jouissance of logos. It is an obligation linked to the imperative that we must use a succession of representations (a logic time) to help conceive of how the subject of the unconscious deploys itself in a tridimensionality. This helps explain how there are certain subjective effects linked to the changes of subjective places. We have to borrow from language in order to give a representation of the structure as a continuity and to represent within it a succession. Because it exists in effect of the real of Φ, phallic jouissance is modalized in two ways: as permitted and as forbidden. JΦ forbidden is tied to a jouissance of the Other (JO).

From the point of view of jouissance, the non-closure of the symbolic takes form as jouissance of the Other. Such a jouissance consists in a forcing of phallic jouissance in an effort to add something which the subject continues to think is lacking. It is the way the subject tries to give consistency to the Other and to make it exist in an effort to complete a narcissistic image. The subject is trapped in an unconscious movement that pushes the subject to annul herself in a masochistic fantasy and to use it to satisfy a want to have a value.

JΦ forbidden is realized when the subject forces, in an imaginary way, the existence of the Other by becoming an object for the Other. It is the way the subject tries to give body to the Other in an effort to give consistency to an image. By passing

50 The discourse of the hysteric and jouissance

through the suffering of the fellow, the subject enjoys their own self-cancellation and comes to value it highly. It is a masochistic jouissance that reproduces the position of being the one who, in a fantasy, is favored by the Other.

Jouissance of sense has to do with a subjective knowledge of where the subject is situated with regard to the three aspects (R, S, I) of the paternal function. The subject always knows, without necessarily understanding, where she is situated in relation to the Other as either imaginary or as symbolic. The topological representation of the spaces of the subject is inseparable from discourse as the ensemble of the indications of modalities of existence of this function as a function of naming. I propose to write jouissance of sense as $J\Psi$. This helps us specify that it is a jouissance of speech. Jouissance of speech is linked to how an unconscious arrangement of signifiers appears in relation to the positions of the subject in a fantasy as different types of knowledge. In giving a situation to the lack fundamental to S_1 as having meaning and signification, S_2 effectively redoubles a lack in S_1. This signifying movement is written: $(S_1)S_1 \rightarrow S_2$. From this, we can also say that $J\Phi$ permitted is experienced as a surplus of existence as a result of its connection to signifiers of desire.

The factor to emphasize here is that the jouissance of the Other does not exist. Because of this, it is modalized into an impossibility unfolding in an infinite horizon coextensive to the supposition of an absolute jouissance. The closure of this jouissance takes on an imaginary consistency. This tells us that jouissance is not something that exists as a being. Jouissance is an effect of the signifying structure of speech. It exists as a movement of signifiers marked by the subjective singularity of accepting or transgressing the symbolic law of the unconscious. One of the meanings of jouissance is that it is a substitute for a loss that never ceases to regenerate the lack. This implies that all subjects belong to the same space, but they are differentiated by the way the subject uses the same space.

Notes

1 As new knowledge, this S_2 appears to both castrate the master and overcome the father, whom she confuses. The hysterical subject wants to save the father from his own impotency.
2 This is linked to the idea of that the way to have the love of Frau K is to turn on her father (a man of means) as a man without means. Sigmund Freud, "Fragment of an Analysis of a Case of Hysteria (1905 [1901])," in *A Case of Hysteria: Three Essays on Sexuality and Other Works: 1901–1905*, ed. and trans. James Strachey, The Standard Edition of the Complete Psychological Works of Sigmund Freud, vol. 7 (London: Vintage, 2001 [1905]), 1–122.

Chapter 16

All-phallic space/non-all phallic space

What is meant here by 'same space'? With *same space*, we are now close to what Lacan found when he discovered the topological structure of the unconscious and what the psychoanalyst Bursztein made more precise by showing the interrelation between the moebian structure of the unconscious and the borromean knot of the unconscious, that is, between castration (lack) and fantasy (jouissance).[1] Namely, we belong to a structure that has two spatialities: all-phallic and non-all phallic.[2] In the all-phallic space, there is one signifier that fulfills the space and determines all the other signifiers. This signifier is written: Φ. In the non-all phallic space, there is a signifier that shows the lack of meaning and inconsistency in the Other, which compels the subject to put another signifier to it. It is written: S(Ø). These two signifiers are characteristic of the two spaces to which all speaking beings belong. I borrow from Bursztein the term *bispatiality* to help conceptualize how such a space is not two things but one thing moving in a continuous dynamic. Lacan's matheme for sexuation shows that Φ and S(Ø) *induce* two major modalities of jouissance: jouissance of logos and jouissance of body.

Placing the accent on *induce* helps bring us nearer to how bispatiality works or not for the subject as an alterity. This alterity is relevant from the way the subject, by means of fantasizing an exteriority, perceives sex as missing in the unconscious image of the body and what in the signifier is lacking as jouissance. One of the meanings of this alterity is that for each sex, the 'other sex' is lacking as jouissance. To say that women are only in the non-all phallic space or that men are only in the all-phallic space supposes that regions of incest do not exist in a woman. For the psychoanalyst, incest (what Lacan calls *sexual relation*) refers only to the way a subject tries in a fusional way to make the Other exist. It is in coextension with the emergence of the lost jouissance of the maternal body the moment the subject passes into language. Incest is a fantasy around an object that is a metaphor of the presence of the Other. What is called 'masculine', 'feminine', 'passive', or 'active' refers only to the fact that we belong to a space characterized by two distinct continuums.[3] Because of this, we participate in this space with different modalities of castration by alternating elements of lack: mark in signifier and lack in jouissance.

Let us clarify that the space where there is jouissance of logos is where it is possible to say that there is signification and meaning. The space where there is a

DOI: 10.4324/9781003366096-16

jouissance of body is tied to resonances of an absence in the Other, which is lacking. We obtain one of our definitions of signifier. Signifier means jouissance. This is why we can also say that it is an incorporated word.

This helps us make more precise the situation of jouissance in the all-phallic space and the non-all phallic space. The question as to the positions of the signifier (the x's in Lacan's matheme) will now be a question as to the way a subject accesses or bypasses the lack in the signifier according to modalities of castration. Another meaning of bispatiality may be expressed as follows: the signifying structure of speech is a double structure of lack. The structure is transmitted as a difference with no consistency, in the sense of an incompletion. As a result, the difference between the two spaces has no presence in itself. We can only say that it exists. It says nothing about which signifiers a subject will extract in reply to an experience of a jouissance felt as a missing fusion. We cannot say which signifiers the subject will extract from the demand of the Other's speech in the effort to generate the meaning and objects of jouissance needed to support the $-\varphi$ (S_2) by representing the first signifiers (S_1) as empty of jouissance. The statement of Newtown helps us here: *hypotheses non fingere.*

This is relevant from the continuum hypothesis of the unconscious. We can neither prove nor refute the statements of the subject. We can only say that they satisfy a choice by putting an equivalence to what is fundamentally unsayable.[4] Let us recall that the appearance of груша in the case of the Wolf Man is intimately connected to the way he hypothesizes the existence of the possibility of castration as a reality in the present. With respect to infantile sexuality, Freud found that the thing is not equivalent to the loss of the presence of the mother. Infantile sexuality is only a result of how the structure is transmitted as castration through a principle of the interdiction of incest. The structure is transmitted as a hole that the subject experiences as a lack. The retroactive effect of language is always there, but Freud insists that there is nothing that allows us to suppose that the 'origin' of castration is attributed to the young subject's imaginary. The young subject is compelled to subjectivize it *by a* lack in order to make it exist and give it consistency. One can start to see how thinking sex is linked to body can lead one to a jouissance of the body where God has not yet left.

It is difficult to perceive that the missing jouissance is what does not pass to the signifier. The signifiers 'man'/'woman' are in effect of this irreducible jouissance, which has no signifier and no signification in itself. The 'other sex' is not an opposite. It takes the form of a jouissance forbidden to the subject because the signifiers 'man'/'woman' are continuously emptied by the turning points of speech. It is true that the signifiers 'man'/'woman' may seem to take on an appearance of simplicity (they may seem to form an empty set calling for further distinctions). But we cannot elide this fact: the signifying movement is always separated from its origin. Because of this, the signifying movement is inseparable from a principle of an obligation to separate. The subject is obliged to construct a fantasy in order to make a hypothesis on the existence of a subjective position separated from object. The subject needs to make a hypothesis on the existence of a reality in which there

All-phallic space/non-all phallic space   53

is nothing impossible about it and which, as a result, is brought into harmony with all logical systems. For such a construction to hold up, one must submit oneself to a name. This is not merely a theoretical issue. It touches upon how a symptom expresses a tying together of the effort and a lack emerging from the synthesis of the ego in the subjective necessity to flee from anxiety.

This point must be emphasized. There are many interpretations of how psychoanalysis formulates differences between sex and gender and of Lacan's 'formula' of sexuation. A fundamental difference exists between the fact of belonging to the same space concerning hypotheses on the existence of a subject, which obliges us to assign conventional names, and the phenomena of the emergence of a perception of structure. What is irreducible in this is not language effects but that no subject has complete and free access to language. Repression is affirmed from psychoanalytic experience. At a certain point, *the subject comes to silence*. The point at which the one saying cannot say otherwise implies that it is not merely a repression at work but more precisely, that what returns us to a repression is something irreducible to a point or to an extension. In other words, there is a formal renunciation always different to a repression. In effect, what we call 'woman'/'man' is connected to the ways the subject will come to call itself 'a man' or 'a woman' from within variations of jouissance characterized by two continuums, which are S_1 and S_2. There are no antinomies here.

Regarding structure, we have, effectively, no other perceptible spaces than those organized by the signifier. Still, there is nothing preventing us from thinking about continuous spaces. To ensure the hypothesis of '*continuation*', the ensemble of all continuations is limited to being imagined in the scopic and in the imaginary. For the signifier, what seems essential is that we can form new bodies by bringing this and that part up to it to say we continue it. But at a certain point, one cannot name it or say it. There will always be this gap.

We are often guilty of expecting a child to know definitions and to know that sometimes definitions are also things called axioms. The psychoanalyst is concerned only with how a subject replies to the lack. The age makes no fundamental difference as to the question of how a subject will come to transfer an imaginary to what, for a moment, makes an ensemble with the real, which cannot be imagined or fantasized. Whether a child is named 'boy' or 'girl' makes no difference as to the way the young subject grasps the unity felt as a missing fusion with the maternal body and makes it a representative of an 'original' element. What comes to make a fundamental difference in subjective existence is the certitude of the one of the structure that one has (or does not have, such as in psychosis), opening the possibility to add dimension to subjectivity.

One can start to see that Lacan must identify the unconscious to variations of space in order to try to convey how jouissance is appearing and working as the basis of the unconscious. The variations in jouissance refer to the variations of the effects of the modifications of the signifying movement, which constitute the borders of the object (a) within the borromean space of representation.[5] With his discovery of the topological structure of the unconscious, Lacan gets ahold of the fact that all variations of jouissance effect all variations of (R), (S), (I). The important point here is that (R, S, I) is internal to a signifier. A modality of jouissance is in itself a pure differential of a passage between signifier and jouissance expressing the various equivalences, which take the forms of satisfactions/dissatisfactions. This is why I propose the hypothesis that the real of the subject is the covariation between jouissance and structure.

Because what differs in the form of the 'other sex' is marked with an irreducible difference in jouissance, one fantasizes the lack in signifier by transforming it into an object of all. What makes a difference in the question of how a subject receives a nomination and takes it as an assignation to a gender is how the knot (R, S, I) is transmitted continuously as a hole. That the situation of signifiers in the borromean knot is inscribed on the edges of the consistencies implies that the fourth term is the names-of-the-father. This helps us perceive that the names-of-the-father is a principle of differentiation, supporting the transmission of castration. This is why it is not an issue of a sort of power linked to a single signifier but rather of how signifier one and a plurality of signifiers of high value enable or not a construction of a fantasy (a knotting that functions as a structure of metaphor). This simply means that whether a subject has heard or not that she has received a name comes down to what is inscribed in consistency. *Consistency is the basis of nomination, not creation.*

Indeed, there are an indefinite number of borromean knots. Of all the ways of knotting, the triskele is the one from which we borrow the least. Now, we can say that consistency is the *unary trait*. From each one, the subject borrows only a single mark and adds a desire. For Freud, this desire will become the possibility of identification and more precisely, a third identification he calls the desire of the hysteric. For Lacan, the necessity of the transmission of structure as castration implies a minimal consistency, allowing for an ongoing reformulation of how the structure of identification is put into place. I identify this necessity to the triskele. It ek-sists as an effect of a retroaction of jouissance. The following figure helps show this:

 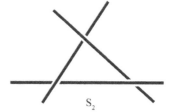

The equivalence between structure and topology that Lacan establishes in *L'étourdit* effectively gives S_2 a new situation.[6] Henceforth, the triskele ek-sists to the subject as a potentiality and a principle of internal finality inherent to the structure. Starting from there, a subject can move to designate to herself the signifier that grasps the dimension of real and which exceeds any symbolic language or imaginary identification. This move is a nomination realizing transformations of signifiers of high value in symbolic namings that limit jouissance. One gives what one does not have.

Notes

1 Bursztein, *Un lexique de topologie Subjective*.
2 This is why psychoanalysis does not speak of the human being but of speaking beings. Further, this is why the psychoanalytical field cannot speak of the unconscious as having a man part and a woman part. It is an epistemological error.
3 This is how I interpret the moebian structure of the unconscious and the way it realizes itself as different to itself.
4 This comes close to Gödel's deduction concerning the formally undecidable. Kurt Gödel, *On Formally Undecidable Propositions of Principia Mathematica and Related Systems*, trans. B. Meltzer (New York: Dover Publications, 1992).
5 The borromean structure of the unconscious means that we start from the hypothesis that the object (a) is linked to a neighboring of the three dimensions, (R), (S), (I), of the structure.
6 That is, he shows the modal existence of real.

Chapter 17

Letters and body

I must return to 'choice' in nomination. There is a difference between the nomination of 'boy' or 'girl' emerging from the speech of the maternal Other and 'man'/'woman' existing to the subject as a choice in two major modalities of jouissance: jouissance of logos and jouissance of body. Here, my topic widens and is more obscure and more difficult to speak about with respect to this.

We have established that nomination is a process of privation. It is an unconscious symbolic nomination implying a nomination to a symbolic. Nomination to a symbolic in turn implies the necessity to name, that is, to give an existence to that which has no being. Naming gives an effect of adding a dimension to subjectivity. By nominating the subject 'a boy' or 'a girl', the choice in one does not go without a privation in the form of the 'other sex' ('girl' for the boy and 'boy' for the girl). Because we cannot escape the fact that choosing one of the two happens from within the signifying structure of speech, we cannot avoid the fact that the two are chosen. In hearing the voice of the word when the signifier is spoken, the place of the two major signifiers seems formally undecidable and as a result, indefinitely interchangeable.[1] In other words, the subject hears that they are spoken by the Other, but she cannot yet say what this nomination is or what it is made of. The subject does not know what to couple nomination with. As a result, the subject is compelled to make a difference.

In order to pass to the place where the subject can construct a fantasy and move to put it into place, it is necessary that the subject perceive a formal cut between jouissance and signifier. A formal rejection is something different than a repression. To support the phallic function as a function of real, the law must transform to a metaphor of the law. The status of the knowledge has to change to a hole in knowledge, allowing the subject to think words are linked to contingency. The One saying effectively transforms a word that is heard to a voice that is listened to or not. In this way, nomination allows a subject to introduce symbolic names that limit the subject in her or his jouissance. It seems that the symbolic nomination moves to an imaginary nomination, enabling the subject to make a connection between the real and the symbolic. It implies access to a position of limitation of the phallic imperative, opening a possible grasp of the symbolic function of the father.[2] It is a kind of symbolic apperception of structure.

DOI: 10.4324/9781003366096-17

The extension of nomination in the imaginary shows that the gesture towards grasping has the same value for the little girl and the little boy. By this, I mean that, from the point of view of the subject as unsayable and not knowing to what nomination is tied, the importance lies in generating the concept of a referent. Symbolic nomination does not in itself make a reference to a boundary by isolating what is inside and what is outside it. In order to specify another set of relations, *the emergence of a body of reference*, or a space of reference as a closed figure, is required. The importance of this event, which is linked to the introduction of a rival, is registered by the effects of the process of identification. This move to the imaginary helps the subject to create a separated space from the symbolic and the real. Starting from there, certain effects of the imaginary are coextensive with a kind of putting forward of two places. There is an acknowledging of a deprivation and a move towards each of them being completely independent of the other. The interrelations between these two places help a subject to realize a symbolic reference to the name in each situation as a different to the One saying. In this sense, such a separated space will extend to supporting a realization of its potentiality as a singular universality irreducible to an all.

When we shift the accent to a subjective position separated from object choice, we are near another change in the status of the knowledge that emerges as a result of a move to nomination in the imaginary. The hole in knowledge changes to the metaphor of the place of the law and a place where desire originates. This gives a certain affective depth and existence to an object, which enables the subject to perceive a distance and look for signifiers that make sense for her or him alone. Letters designate the places of the metaphor of the body of the Other. It is difficult to grasp that such a body does not exist, especially when nomination in the imaginary shows that the Other and the other sex emerge together. Because this body does not exist, there is an immediate overlap in the form of a *vocare* to a supposed limitless jouissance. Such a jouissance, which is impossible and supposed to the signifier 'father', compels each one to imagine a real father. It is crucial here to grasp that the irreducibility of the imaginary is situated in the real. Because of this, there is a subjective push to the 'woman'. By supporting the idea that she has a privileged jouissance, the subjective need to imagine a real father—in the same moment—is a renunciation of the loss of the maternal body and an identification with the father. What this means may be expressed as follows: for this non-existent body that the subject experiences in the sense of an incompleteness, a need to make the Other exist arises. In a certain way, the subject needs to call upon 'woman' so that there may be the possibility of a common enjoyment, an enjoyment that is one and which defends the subject against abandonment. We are compelled to accept that the situation of the imaginary induces real images that exist to the subject. Because they have no possible representation, they can only be met with in anguish, in delusions, and in uncanniness. Repression does not go without introducing an ideal in the form of one flesh.

Experience in the clinic shows that the emergence of the existence of the subject has a motive, a referent, and signifiers by which it has been marked. The signifier is not only transmitted. Let us recall Freud's example of the 'glance on the nose' in his essay on *Fetishism*.[3] Even if what is involved in the signifier is a changing sense ('a shine on the nose' changes to 'a look at the nose'), it is the same. The changing of the position of the signifier 'nose' leads the subject to the gaze and keeps him situated under it. Here, the movement of the signifying articulation functions to dynamize the organization of a fantasy into a reality. It is necessary to incorporate the mark in signifier as an otherness to what is said. This tells us that in a certain way, the signifier transmits nothing other than what is lacking in the subject as jouissance, which implies a fundamental lack of guarantee in the Other. This double structure seems to be the object that causes the spaces of appearance in subjectivity. That is, (R), (S), (I) appear like dimensions of space. The important factor here is that, as a result of its tie to the function of logos, the signifier exists as a position of semblant. This existence opens the possibility for the subject to divide the subjective space into three spatial consistencies. Effectively, the signifier is articulated through a kind of triple finality, which are regions of jouissance, that realizes itself as a holey structure through which the subject must pass.

Where topology makes a deep step is in regard to the question of how the subject of the unconscious is existing. My hypothesis is that the existence of the unconscious supposes a writing close to mathematical writing. It exists as ensembled letters, designating the places where the unconscious appears and is working. When listening to how a subject is trying to grasp, explain, and understand their symptoms—that is, trying to interpret the contingencies of their existential positions—it becomes impossible to deny that all the rhetorical procedures and all the logic have only the means of a neighborhood to help give some expressions. It is because one element follows another that there exists a link, to which we are called to listen. The importance lies in the *notion of neighborhood*. In the clinic, this has been called 'free association'.

Further, we learn from the topology of the signifying movement that the number of substitutions for a signifier maximally permitted is one. It is difficult to deny that the word 'if' takes on a value that is fundamentally different when it is replaced by the letter 'p'. The point here is relevant from the writing that the unconscious supposes. Writing is not a condition of existence; it is a hypothesis on existence. In psychoanalysis, writing refers to unconscious interpretations of subjective position. It is not a search for the essence, such as it is in philosophy. Because the letter can be designated, the status of subjective knowledge changes. Starting from this, it is easier to grasp (but difficult to accept) that letters do not have meaning. They empty jouissance of consistency. This implies that letters have a function. From them, we obtain extensions of jouissance that have an effect of another jouissance, that of body without object. Lacan calls this *substance jouissante*.[4]

It is not easy to perceive that there is something that cannot be written into Lacan's matheme for sexuation. It is nonetheless implied and goes without saying. An interpretation of the situation of letters helps us interpret that the two major modalities induced (jouissance of logos and jouissance of body) are inseparably linked to a substance in the methodology. I associate this to what Lacan calls the 'other' jouissance. I prefer to retain 'feminine' to help keep the referent to a methodological necessity inherent to psychoanalysis as generating a particular science.[5] Subjective topology is a question of defining something in relation to where the subject is situated, and it is a way of replying in jouissance. This is why subjective topology makes a different step. It enables us to realize that conceptualizations of the difference between sexes or genders are not necessary to the ways a subject is always knotting and unknotting. In a certain way, it helps us avoid basing ourselves on ideologies and assuming idealisms regarding how each subject formulates their singular subjectivity within a collective. We can now clarify our earlier hypothesis that sex is an invention of body by adding that sex is not linked to body.

In the unconscious, there is neither 'yes' nor 'no'. Starting from there, we know that the relation to the 'other sex' appears in the emergence of singular elements extracted from a world of language that carries the fact that it is not a totality. The 'body' that feels through anxiety, symptoms, and inhibitions is situated in the tridimensionality of the structure immanent to language. This implies a problematic that remains open and which is not at all easy to either show or give an analytic description of.

Notes

1 The psychoanalytic formally undecidable is close to what Gödel demonstrated with respect to how it functions to satisfy an axiom of choice in relation to the continuum hypothesis.
2 In *Encore*, Lacan indexes this to 'dieu-dire'. Lacan, *On Feminine Sexuality: The Limits of Love and Knowledge*.
3 Sigmund Freud, "Fetishism," in *The Future of an Illusion: Civilization and Its Discounters and Other Works: 1927–1931*, ed. James Strachey, The Standard Edition of the Complete Psychological Works of Sigmund Freud, vol. 21 (London: Vintage, 2001 [1927]), 149–57, 152.
4 Lacan, *On Feminine Sexuality: The Limits of Love and Knowledge*, 24.
5 This necessity is linked to the activity of finding equivalences on the basis of the nonrelation to the being of the sexual relation. Such an activity has to do with to what Freud highlighted, which is the importance of the unconscious equivalence between the mother and the virgin in the oedipal movements of the subject.

Chapter 18

Signifier and symptom

In *Inhibitions, Symptoms, and Anxiety*, Freud got ahold of the fact that the symptom is articulated to inhibitions, symptoms, and anxiety, which are like dimensions of space. This is a consequence of the fact that in itself, the symptom has no representation. The difficulty here is linked to *urverdrangung*, a first repression, which is supposed to remain a problematic. It ensures not only the return of the repressed but also that the return of the repressed is an answer of the subject to a feeling of the lack. An unconscious image of narcissism will build itself by the efforts the subject takes to restore a fusional feeling of unity to his subjective perception of body. This is why, for example, obsessional symptoms manifest in forms of guilt. Speech is necessary to the incarnation of repression as the ambiguity of an image. For the psychoanalyst, speech is the first category. Starting from this, impossibility is not only to do with something that one cannot say otherwise; it is also that the one saying cannot avoid coming to *a point of no-saying*. This supposition belongs to all those who speak.[1] For example, in the case of Little Hans, the signifier *widdler* is indexed to a function of a saying by the mother and a saying by the father. The parental sayings, the 'of course, why?' and the 'yes, of course' help set him about his task.[2] The sayings are, in a sense, obliging the young scientist to go about making a selection of innumerable facts offered to his curiosity. In other words, he is compelled to look for signifiers that will make sense for him by giving meaning and signification to the symbolic existence of the law. Because he is compelled to make a choice from within the enumeration of places close to where a *widdler* seems to appear (if only by thinking it), the choice is always a sacrifice. The aforenamed real makes sense for Little Hans. Let us posit that this extraction of signifiers is not the same as when there is an element introduced into the real (that is, when there is an extraction of letters that obliges the subject to resituate jouissance), but it is a sense all the same. It is crucial that Little Hans's fear of crossing is linked to the certainty that a horse will bite him.

It is not merely that Little Hans can't avoid thinking it. My hypothesis is that, for Little Hans, *widdler* is also an instantiation of a letter. The moment Little Hans has to *widdle*, the signifier passes to an element of jouissance, inducing a feeling of a fusional unity with the parental Other. The letter *r* jointly induces an appearance attached to the connection of the body of the mother and the possibility of being

DOI: 10.4324/9781003366096-18

in the likeness of his father. The moment signifier passes to jouissance, the letter is detached of body and is returned as lack, bringing about a desire.

In a certain way, renunciation is inseparable from making repression the locus of origin. This is how Little Hans grasps the appearance of a lack of a penis on the body of the mother in making of it a mythical evocation of a first repression he *thinks as a source*. Starting from there, he can set about loving it. He makes an imaginary interpretation that helps ensure *the supposition* of a lack is that which guarantees there is meaning. Without it, there is no possibility for creating a sense of law generating a prohibition of transgression. It is important to grasp and perceive that incest takes on an equivalence of an abolition of all sense. The subject needs a metaphor of jouissance to support a feeling of having a place rightfully his own. Little Hans needs to infer that *his mother must have a widdler like a horse* in order to have a large return, which is the identification of himself with his mother and with a form of the image made in the likeness of a signifier. By functioning as a replacement in a fantasy, the fear of horses is a sacrifice by which anxiety recedes into the background. In a certain way, Little Hans's inhibition at going into the street where he is sure he will be bitten by horses testifies to the fact that at a particular moment, elements in a signifying chain that are forbidden, impossible, and therefore supposedly rejected by it are not able to be reintroduced by another chain of signifiers. There is no substitute for it. This means that castration does not appear governed by mere caprice of nature or by an intelligence conscious of an end to be attained.

Interpretations as to the movements of jouissance within subjective positions help explain that the all-phallic and non-all phallic spaces are in no case able to create a unity. It is much harder to show since the difficulty seems to lie in this: we cannot avoid to think of a hole. Indeed, this is related to the need of the subject to think the body as a hole. Symptoms are tied to the passes of speech aiming at spaces emptied of jouissance. There is no way to make a demonstration of it except to borrow in order to make a reference under which the subject exists. This tells us that phallic jouissance implies choosing only one trait (some one) that has no reference to the Other and which does not need to be guaranteed by the instance of the Other. The jouissance of the Other implies a jouissance of body but a jouissance of the Other that has been lost/repressed.

It is difficult to give up the idea that sex is linked to body, but this is precisely what psychoanalytic experience obliges of us. Letters are only a testimony of a presence of a jouissance of the mother-child tie that has been lost. For example, when the child perceives the mother as pleased with her. They are not written on the body. Letters are extracted from a perception of a lack in body as an effect of speaking. *Letters* help name an effect of speech that cannot be recreated in a fantasy. They are real and have an effect of a real. They do not exist in a signifying articulation; they have no physical characteristic. The existence of letters is simply that of a differential feature to jouissance and signifier.

It seems that castration also has the support of a jouissance linked to letters and is thus removed from giving it a reference to an image of body. Castration is not a physical principle. When Freud attributed 'penis envy' to women, it had to do with how repression is brought about by a double movement of the subject. By this, I mean that when the subject passes into language, which is also an assumption of castration, the difference between the organ and the symbolic phallus appears. This difference is in coextension to a knowledge that the symbolic phallus exists, but it is not possible to put any concrete content to represent it. Facing this point of the lack of an imaginary agent is what psychoanalysis calls 'the penis'. It is a fundamental confrontation with a lack in all. Experience shows that this does not mean that because a person is a woman she is defined by an envy of the penis or that an individual who has a penis does not experience it. The tendency towards explaining penis envy by general considerations of it being linked to an epiphany of an organ, like the oracle of Delphi, remains prevalent. Why, then, is it considered a mark of femininity?

Notes

1 This is why in psychoanalysis, we say that the field is concerned with the speaking being. It does not study the human being. It is therefore not an anthropology, sociology, and much less a psychology of the mind.
2 Sigmund Freud, "Analysis of a Phobia in a Five-Year-Old Boy," in *Two Case Histories: "Little Hans" and the "Rat Man": 1909*, ed. and trans. James Strachey, The Standard Edition of the Complete Psychological Works of Sigmund Freud, vol. 10 (London: Vintage, 2001 [1909]), 1–150, 7–9.

Chapter 19

Mark in signifier

The way the subject is marked by a signifier is woven from three movements: a parental context (where there are various markers expressing jouissance, anxiety, suffering, tenderness, and more); an obligation to pass into language in order to be extended into a horizon of value (this is linked to the function of the symbolic phallus as designating the places where there is no access to the Other's desire); and by a unary trait that extends as the subject's imaginary. These movements are inseparable from the fundamental irreducibility of the lack in jouissance relevant from speech. Transference teaches us that the neurotic uses the imaginary to induce a reference to the Other in order to give herself as an object of demand. In this way, the subject seeks to cancel the Other's desire in an effort to complete an image of narcissism.

Let us go back to jouissance as a differential of a signifying movement. An element that subjective topology brings forth is that jouissance exists as a continuous movement of a spatiality different to itself. The moment the signifier passes to an element of jouissance, inducing a flourishing of three types of jouissance around an object in a fantasy, there is an immediate induction of spaces separated from those regions of jouissance and from the signifying movement as separated from its source. These three spaces separated from object by a subjective distance are the real of the real, the real of the imaginary, and the real of the symbolic. To these spaces, I associate a neighborhood of real. They are constitutive of the modality of *substance jouissante* in which the subject of speech is occurring and working to generate a dynamic. This is what Lacan called a 'speaking body'.[1] I interpret this as follows: the emergence of a structure of body is marked. It is on the basis of a subject's jouissance that the unconscious is existing.

This implies that jouissance is not only a substance different from the signifier; it is also the modality indexing the real of speech. It is something felt without a perception of object in expressing itself under variations of forms of satisfactions/dissatisfactions. This helps explain why in the rotations of unconscious discourses, an interpretive question coming from the analyst can help the analysand

DOI: 10.4324/9781003366096-19

catch a glimpse of the signifiers that are annulling. Such variations are bounded to a knowledge that jouissance is not forever. The moment there is a disappearance of jouissance, an equivalent to the lack comes, enabling the possibility for satisfaction. It corresponds to the fall of the phallic function, namely, to the detumescence of the penis.

I associate this differential relevant from the movements of jouissance to a collapse of the knotting in which the retroaction of jouissance immediately restores the subject to a lack. Let us emphasize that this lack is not nothing. This lack is a call to resituate jouissance, effectively putting into place a fantasy. This comes close to what Leibniz conceived regarding how the coexistence of space and body is linked to extensions as subjective deductions.[2] The field of possible opened unto the subject is linked to the way the subject will resituate jouissance in reply to the ways he or she will interpret the contingencies of unconscious sayings. I associate this call to resituate and put into place jouissance to the *triskele*, a minimum consistency that ek-sists to the subject as a potentiality of knotting. It is a principle of transmission effectively generating lack under three modalities: deprivation, frustration, and castration. These three modalities bring forth an interrelation where the subjective space is shown, opening unto a possibility of extracting new signifiers of high value from the infinite of the speech transmitted by inducing a neighboring with Φ. The following figure helps show this:

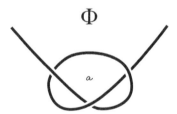

The difficulty is to grasp and accept that the transmission of speech does not go without implying a lack in meaning in the Other and an emptying of jouissance. Let us recall that Φ is a statement of the subject. One of the meanings of Φx may be expressed as follows: it is impossible as a cause. Because of this, the statements of the subject (such as 'there is no' and 'there exists one') reveal the necessity to produce a discourse. This is linked to how the subject is specifying what demands to be singled out by speaking.

Yet, as Lacan's matheme for sexuation shows, the subject can neither have all the signifiers nor put all the signifiers in exactly the same place. It is not a question of seeing where the object (a) is. It is a *question of listening to how it is emerging*—in act and in potential—as a knotting. That is, as a subject of speech. Lacan situates the letters outside the knot. This is important because it relies on an appearance of a separated space as a kind of non-space hole (an (a)).[3]

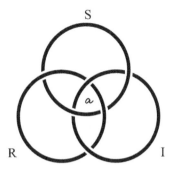

Let us distinguish repetitions. There are two: jouissance linked to signifiers (where there is signification and meaning) and jouissance linked to letters (where there is an effect of body without meaning). If one bases oneself on an imaginary of drawings, one misses the fact that the knotting is also an assumption of the lack of duality called 'body' and 'intellect'. In this way, the borromean knot is a structure of metaphor in which desire is no longer defined as a metonymy of a lack to be. Desire is reformulated as a capacity to move to an unknown point without losing oneself in wandering.

This brings us to a question of envy in excess. It seems to me that by 'penis envy', Freud came near to this problematic in his essay 'The psychogenesis of a case of homosexuality in a woman'. It would take us too to far from our task here to enter into a discussion about paranoia. It is sufficient to state that the paranoia of neurotics shows us that jealousy is necessary for participating in the social bond. We call jealousy a metaphor of envy, but its position is linked to a particular one. Jealously is like envy in its good aspect. Envy in excess is something different than jealousy. It implies a different position characterized by a dual fought between two under the gaze of an unrecognized third. In this relation, the other being who is supposed to possess this object, an object that is the one stolen by this other being, has a lack that is making the subject, 'the me', suffer. By her very presence, the other being steals from the subject the object that matters most, which is no other than the imaginary phallus as the agent of privation and frustration. The subject can be in possession of it only one at a time.[4]

The return of excess in envy implies another small other, a third one in the form of a surplus of existence. But this surplus comes to function in an outstanding way. Because the mirror of the Other has already constructed an image for 'me' of the fellow being, this surplus works as a figure of a sort of super ideal. Until that point, the mirror of the Other worked as an ideal complementary because it relied on the image of the other as captivating and as giving support insofar as it is around him (the father of reality) that a narcissistic identification is formulated. In envy in excess, the phallus seems to appear twice over in the imaginary. It is now a fundamental lack in being and a lack in depth that are cloaked in an imaginary, operant unity. In this way, the fantasy attributes the autoerotic object to the other in the effort to bring about a direct equivalence between satisfaction and dissatisfaction by cancelling the other from their own fantasy. In this way, it is something like an attempt to annihilate the subject by forcing a changing of the status of the subject's jouissance. The one who provokes envy changes to being the one who is forced to envy, that is, deprived and frustrated of the love and affection otherwise possessed.

The philosophical statement that there exists a lesbian phallus compels psychoanalysis to make a deeper distinction between the signifier 'lesbian' and the phallus.[5] By now, it is sufficient to state that the phallus is not a signifier. It does not function like a signifier because it has no content or representation in itself. Nomination helps us perceive that the Other emerges in what appears in the form of the other sex. It is experienced as a necessary privation modalizing under three elements of lack: deprivation, frustration, and symbolic castration. In the psychoanalytical field, the signifier 'lesbian' is a surplus of existence situated in the phallic space. To try to deploy the signifier in an attempt to hypothesize the all-phallic space as the condition for existence effectively forces a consistence to the difference between the jouissance of logos and the jouissance of body. The jouissance of the body indicates that there is no possibility to constitute a set that would contain all women. There is no universal of castration. This does not mean that because a person is a lesbian, she is not a woman. Or that because a person is a woman, she can be only with a man or with another woman in a masculine way in her everyday sexual life. What Lacan called *heteros* does not refer to a way of acting or to sexual practices. It is a way of assuming a substantial identity through an assumption of a symbolic nomination and an acceptance of an unconscious image as always lacking.

What subjective topology brings forth is that jouissance is existing under the form of a singularity within each element in the world. This form of referent, which we now call 'woman', only exists through an interpretation of letters and writing. It also brings forth that the 'phallus' becomes desirable through the desire of someone else.

We must therefore appreciate what in Lacan is extracted from Freud and made more precise. However much of an emphasis Lacan placed on a relation to the signifier, he nevertheless managed to show that the putting in place of a fantasy does not necessarily require a paternal intervention. To put it another way, choice in jouissance is a path that is only the business of the subject.

Notes

1 Lacan, *On Feminine Sexuality: The Limits of Love and Knowledge*.
2 Gottfried Wilhelm Leibniz, "On Body and Force, Against the Cartesians (May 1702)" and "On the Nature of Body and the Laws of Motion (ca 1678–82)," in *Philosophical Essays*, trans. Roger Ariew and Daniel Garber (Indianapolis: Hackett Publishing Company, 1989), 250–56.
3 In *L'étourdit*, Lacan calls this *n'espace*. Lacan, "L'étourdit," 449–95.
4 Let us notice that the insistence on only one subject at a time can have the imaginary phallus is a way to ensure that succession is possible.
5 Butler, *Bodies That Matter: On the Discursive Limits of "Sex"*.

Chapter 20

Sexual difference

A radical alternative

I must now turn to the question of the case. I have refrained from giving my own case examples. This does not merely have to do with my preference to avoid adding to impressions that psychoanalysis is a treatment of pathologies, that it is possible to reduce psychoanalytic practice to a normative form, or that it is based on a high theoretical knowledge. For the psychoanalyst, the symptom is not a pathology. It has to do with what has no representation but demands insistently. Nomination has to do with how meaning, in each case, is a different meaning. As I grasp it, we are in error to use cases as examples. What is possible is to try to extract elements from singularities in cases and try to interpret them on the basis of one's own knowledge acquired in the psychoanalytical experience of the cure. Indeed, analyses of Freud's cases cannot be exhausted.

Let me therefore not delay any further and try to approach the question of imaginary nomination. I am trying to explain how the return of repression is working for the subject of the unconscious. In Freud, it is linked to a second moment in the Oedipus complex. This moment works like a moment of an appeal. In the case of Schreber, his paranoia shows the fact that no other sexual relation except one with God is possible. This impossibility is linked to the fact that he finds himself in the position of God's wife, a true woman, '*while separated in space*'. He remains infinitely close to God but subjected to human laws. It seems that because he is in this place, he is not duped by the activity of naming.[1] He says, 'Certainly not a single soul remained with any awareness of the name under which it had belonged to one or other'.[2] It is important that among all the symbolic names that appear, there is one that he never mentions. He is careful to preserve this one name, placing his statement regarding it in the beginning. It is no other than the name of 'his wife'. At no point does he say it.

My hypothesis is that in psychosis, the subject has not heard that he has received a name. This is not merely a question of repression. It also linked to a formal renunciation. The importance of what Schreber calls *Der ewige Jude* (translated as the Eternal Jew) and the way many other things are called by this name is registered at the form that manifests an existence of body. It is a question, here, of *the wandering*. If all sons are eternal, then the father can neither demand nor require of them a sacrifice. It is no longer 'man' who is divided, but God himself. God's hands are, in a sense, tied. Absolute, unlimited jouissance is no longer his. What

DOI: 10.4324/9781003366096-20

seems to surprise Schreber is not only this but also that the existence of God takes on no injunction. The god who wants him to transform into a woman with corresponding female sexual organs is named Ariman. Schreber notices that, in him, no objection appears. There is no fundamental need on the part of Ariman to make an objection to losing himself in extending to Schreber a part in his body because he has no cause for it. Ariman is also nearly always guaranteed of having the certitude of the one of structure by having all the *voluptuousness*. Schreber notices that the extensions of 'a feeling of soul-voluptuousness' are effectively not always absent/ present in his body. He perceives that God accomplishes an escape from his fate by using his body. Schreber's body is God's immortality.[3]

Let us posit that the existence of Ariman is not separated from the form of the body under which he commands. This wandering thing has no designation through metaphor. As a result, there is no instance introducing a separated name. The jouissance that is supposed as limited has no signifier of the difference. That is, there is no name by which Schreber can call himself, enabling him to perceive the symbolic status of the father. It seems that there is also no symbolic naming that would help remove him from the body jouissance of Ariman. For Schreber, it is extremely difficult, if not impossible, to name himself from within the double structure of lack. He finds himself in the position of god's wife, but it is a god who is in possession of a differentiation in form between 'man', 'woman'. There is no call of a difference between image and form, within which a metaphoric capacity of language extends. In effect, there is no instance of a law helping to limit jouissance, enabling the grasp of a plurality in signifiers of high value specific to him, which allow him to stop wandering in their existence.

My hypothesis is that psychosis is characterized by a lack of a formal cut between signifier and jouissance.[4] I propose the following figure for the psychotic structure:

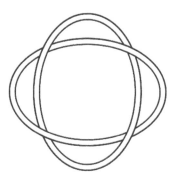

In psychosis, it seems that there is a continuous interpenetrating of signifier and jouissance, of ego and id. This helps to explain that a distinction exists between the way the subject is inhibited by the presence of the Other in psychosis and in neurosis. In psychosis, the subject is woven of a non-differentiated jouissance. The structure realizes itself at most in one consistency characterized by the infinite of signifiers existing in a continuum with the continuity of the gaze. In neurosis, such a formal cut exists, allowing the subject to pass to spaces where the real of sex manifests itself through a differential movement of jouissance. The point to emphasize is that in neurosis, *the knot is differentiated in separated consistencies*, (R), (S), (I), enabling the subject to perceive a causality.

Lacan identified the psychotic structure to the trefoil knot. Today, various interpretations of the borromean knot show a tendency of being led to the supposition that there exists something which might be called an ordinary psychosis. This contains a statement that may be expressed as follows: all speaking beings belong in some way to a psychotic structure. Or to put it differently: psychosis is the name for potentiality. It seems to me that this is an imaginary interpretation overlooking the substance of speech and the function of voice. Further, it misses the question of where the status of knowledge supporting the psychotic structure is situating itself and that of *the active difference* between structure and spaces of representation. It also seems to me that this is a chance to renew and reformulate the concept of transference and how we obtain a notion of function from a neighboring of places.

The case of Schreber brings forth a fundamental feature of the speaking being. It is both the change of status and necessity of *resemblance*. Basing oneself on a static image of the knot misses the fact that Schreber has no image of his own.[5] In a deeper way, such a belief in ordinary psychosis mistakes the borromean knot for the basis of a message. In psychosis, there is a problematic concerning an extension of the real in the imaginary, preventing the subject to realize a differential of space in an imaginary. Unlike what happens in neurosis, where there is capacity of the subject to pass from jouissance of logos to jouissance of body, from jouissance of body to jouissance of logos in a fantasy, this capacity in psychosis seems extremely limited, partialized, or impossible.

To assert an existence—one where it is possible to lay rightful claim to having a value among others with a way to refer its value for another as a unit—the subject needs appearances of separated spaces. The semblant must also move within subjectivity to help activate and enable a capacity of the subject to change positions. We know from experience that changes in position generate meaning and sense and a space for desire. Here, one starts to grasp the importance of an imaginary nomination linked to symbolic names that limit, and why it is also necessary to take account of a return of repression as implying an acceptance or refusal of it.

Notes

1 Daniel Paul Schreber, *Memoirs of My Nervous Illness*,. trans. Ida Macalpine and Richard A. Hunter (New York: New York Review Books, 2000), 10. Following the ways Schreber's links 'rays' to a figure of speech, he perceives that the body he has does not belong to him.
2 Schreber, *Memoirs of My Nervous Illness*, 30.
3 Schreber, *Memoirs of My Nervous Illness*, 166.
4 One notices that there is no space different to an imaginary.
5 This helps explain why in psychosis, there is sometimes an immediate distrust of the image that appears before the subject when looking into a mirror and an inescapable obligation to look in the mirror.

Chapter 21

Return to a remark in signifier

Even if Lacan did not precisely say it in every moment, he grasped that the principle of repression is more fundamental to a 'first' repression or a 'second'. In his seminars on *The Purloined Letter* and *The Instance of the Letter in the Unconscious*, we see that there is a fundamental difference between a repression working on a signifier and a repression linked to an instance when the letter is struck by an impossibility. There is a moment when an element falls outside the signifying movement and cannot reenter because it is effectively subjected to repression. To bring about the possibility of substitution by leaving some signifiers linked together is something different than trying to situate them in the real. One of the meanings of symbolic castration is that all the jouissance cannot be put into the structure. The subject is called to give it a different situation from an extreme minimum, from signifiers marked by a lack in *all*. The discovery of the topological structure of the unconscious helped make this point more precise. This implies that the signifier is also an instantiation of a letter. The letter marks out a place and goes toward the place of the signifier.

Here is where Freud's testimony makes itself felt. He takes seriously the status of his grandson's knowledge and tries to interpret it. In the example of fort/da, we see precisely that the unconscious knowledge of the child consists in the fact that there should be a fundamental disappearance.[1] For example, the child is no longer compelled to cry when the mother is absent, as if she may leave and he would never know if she is coming back. But in a certain way, she is there all the same and never completely gone, even if the mother has gone away. To help put in place its presence and better assure it, there is a formal rejection of the thing. For the object to be present, including when it is felt as absent in body (the mother), it is necessary that there should be a disappearance of jouissance, since this is what henceforth allows him to carry on with finding forms of satisfaction/dissatisfaction. The point is that the imaginary, as something that gives consistency to reality, is metaphorizing the symbolic as making a hole in knowledge by indicating an incompleteness and the missing jouissance of the mother/child tie as a presence that is lacking. Let us propose that the body is not the real of the subject. The real of the subject shows itself through the body and is no doubt felt in the body. The body is where the jouissance is not.

DOI: 10.4324/9781003366096-21

Because there is a repression, there is an investment by an imaginary phallus. What both Freud and Lacan evoke is that something else is involved in the signifier, something that no longer belongs to the appearance of an order of a signifying movement. Once some signifiers are extracted from the maternal discourse, the subject no longer has the others. Analytic experience obliges us to notice that an image always goes with a signifier. It is necessary to take account of how this linkage functions for the subject. Let us also propose that an acceptance of repression is like a symbolic debt. The agent, no more found to be named 'father', accounts in him the debt: for each for each one, 'my' debt is cut so in the same moment, 'my' jouissance should be possible. In a counterintuitive way, this gives castration a kind of support that removes it from the referent to any image of body or some obscure subjective power and indeed, from a paternal intervention. The signifier is liable to take on a dimension of voice in the subject, which means that the signifier is no longer listened to but heard.

Let us now pose a question about the object. How can we say it is characterized? It is situated in speech. The object is characterized by two main modalities: an extraction of signifiers and an extraction of letters. As signifiers, they are what the subject thinks are the demands/desires of the Other. They are *the aim* or *the correspondence*. This helps explain that in a fundamental fantasy, signifiers have to do with the type of object the subject is for her Other. The aim of the subject is to bring about a complete correspondence: a change in sign in the Other with a sign in the real-image. The signifier is articulated to three dimensions: the lack in the Other; perception of a lack; and demands/desires of the Other that insist. Signifiers are extracted following the aim to bring about a harmony among these three facets of lack. Because lack is not in itself an element and by speaking, the signifier is lacking, the transmission of the structure needs support.

Note

1 Sigmund Freud, "Beyond the Pleasure Principle," in *Beyond the Pleasure Principle: Group Psychology and Other Works: 1920–1922*, ed. and trans. James Strachey, The Standard Edition of the Complete Psychological Works of Sigmund Freud, vol. 18 (London: Vintage, 2001 [1920]), 1–6.

Chapter 22

Formations of voice

By trying to explain the link between sex and nomination, I have been trying to answer a question. How does the acceptance of a difference, which has no content and no possible representation, transform the subject? What is fundamentally asked, demanded, and desired of us in the clinic? It is to be in a position of only a listener and to listen to a subject's complaints.[1] In every statement of a situation, there is an unconscious structural conception. In every statement of the subject, there is a more fundamental one not only supporting the possibility to conceive and realize a structure of transmission but also permitting it. There is a process of substitution of signifiers, which is characterized by the fact that at most, only one signifier can substitute at a time. And there is a movement of one consistence to another. It is impossible to avoid that in the two processes, one is bounded to result in something that goes out of sense *as outside* (as a gain in meaning) in linking inside and outside (as a signification resulting in a certain loss of sense). These two modulate the three (R), (S), (I) of the unconscious spaces where the subject is appearing and transforming.

My hypothesis is that this fundamental one is no other than *voice*. The voice emerges out of the speech of the maternal Other and transmits its presence. What psychoanalysis calls 'language' does not transmit the voice immediately or directly, and as such, expresses itself through speech spelling signifiers. Psychoanalytic writing does not express this voice. As a result, writing consists in signifying it under forms of letters, marking jouissance as tied to functions of 'having'. It is sure that this is why a demonstration of the psychoanalytical 'the real' is the most difficult, if not impossible. How to convey letters and signifiers as jouissance effects giving dimension of voice only *one by one*? This is why subjective topology is a methodological necessity and a pure element of psychoanalytical knowledge. At a certain point, the subject comes to a point of silence, a formal gap. Such a gap is articulated to a point of no-saying and a point that cannot be said. One can no less name it than say it. In effect of these two points, the subject is obliged to move to these unknown points, accept them, and carry on one by one. This helps explain why psychoanalysis is characterized by a difference of modalities of infinite, such as the retroaction of jouissance and après-coup.

DOI: 10.4324/9781003366096-22

There is an infinite that has no starting or ending, which characterizes psycho-analytical work as something that is ongoing. And there is an infinite that consists in passing continuously from finite to infinite, infinite to finite. This passage has to do with the ways a subject grasps and perceives the signifiers that matter and which as a result, continuously compel the subject to resituate jouissance. It consists in an interrelation of interpretive cuts and metaphoric interpretations that support a subject in putting into place new situations concerning the statements said in a circle of close ones (what is called a familial).[2] These modalities are themselves induced by the real of the mark of letters. Because of such marks, it seems that the function of the differential of jouissance is constituted across two modalities of the object (a): as lack and as support for the fantasy. This implies that modalities of the object (a) continuously induce a neighborhood of real (characterized as an infinitely close) that implies the existence of a modality of space: the density of One. Such a density is expressed by an alternating of the passes of subjective positions where the moments of lack of jouissance and the finding of signifiers generate jouissance.

The point to emphasize here is the experience of the psychoanalytical cure, where the work is slow, gradual, and not always easy. It is also limited. It has no object other than supporting a subject to move to stand in what her or him alone is desire. Desire is only that which supports an unconscious subject. The articulations of it ties each one to a singular type of destiny that, in returning, situates the subject once more in a path that is only the business of the subject.

What is meant by this? It would be a false reduction to say that either one follows the path of logic or one follows the path of presenting knots and other topological figures. It is a question of trying to present, from one instance to another by means of a choice, how the unconscious is deploying itself without relying on representations of the lack. In this way, as much as is possible, the work stays close to psycho-analytical truth. The moment the subject says a 'yes' or a 'no', there is a deletion of time. To say that the unconscious knows no concept of time is a truth inseparable from the way each subject is in, out, out, in of language/speech, generating a move to give a content to their infantile sexuality. It is not an object of a theory. To reduce oneself to only a listener is to assume a position of a relation to unknown knowledge and to accept to hear the knowledge (known and unknown) resulting from the statements of the analysand. It has nothing to do with power. In going from an other to an other, what exists are formations of voice.

The voice is certainly an enigmatic point. It is sure that regarding voice, we find ourselves confronted to ambiguity. But there is also no secret key to turn, unlocking a window unto its mysteries. We cannot avoid confronting the fact that we always find ourselves as having two supposed to form one flesh. By a voice enunciating a word, we are called to lend our own, 'my', voice to what is fundamentally silent and what is not named in it, in what was stated. In a way, we take the 'voice' as an assignation to a gender. Entering into the 'group' depends on the ways a subject interprets the demands and desires of his or her Other. How a subject incorporates said demands or accepts to leave them concerns the difficulty of symbolic castration. Dropping the imaginary object that the subject uses to add/subtract from a narcissistic image constitutes symbolic castration.

What psychoanalysis calls letter is very near Euler's letter. It is only a way of characterizing voice by its porosity in form by means of a cut into the form. That is, it is only a way of characterizing substance by proximities in densities of matter and spaces empty of matter. Euler calls this thickness and thinness.[3] The *inseparability of two* neighbors psychoanalytic formations of the one of the structure as consisting in a continuous space and in the potential infinity of the elements (R), (S), (I) of the signifying movement. The voice is not a sound, and it is much less an entity. Indeed, there is no way it can have any concrete being because as, Euler beautifully shows, voice is only something that exists as an instance of a formation. In itself, such a moment is in effect of how the mouth is pushing elements through holes and with placements of tongue. Because of this, there is a neighboring of three primary 'vowels': the *e feminine*, the *e masculine*, and *i as pronounced in ich*. He identifies *e feminine* to the letter; it is an effect of speech. The *e masculine* is identified to an intermediate position of mouth. The *i* is identified to a smallness of scope where the use of the tongue helps to narrow as much as possible the cavity of the mouth. Between *e feminine* and *e masculine*, there is no essential difference. The two are irreducible to any sort of presence. Between them there are infinite intermediaries. To go from one to another, it is necessary to use an intermediary.

The way Euler explains to himself the phenomena of voice is with the support of a minimal notion of body. He shows formations of voice as relevant from how language and body are woven of movements through and around holes. The voice empties the dimensions of a signifier, enabling one to move to positions of speech and language—that is, to make a difference and further distinctions. It is something inducing an appeal to interpretation, which is more or less linked to a contingency. This is why it is important to place an accent on a minimal consistence as the fundamental support of the subject. Indeed, the body is not the real of the subject. The real shows itself through body in dimensions of voice unique to each one. The subject experiences letters through body as an ensemble of a real of the real, a real of the symbolic, and a real of the imaginary. The following helps show how the places of the subject are open to the subject:

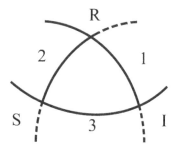

Starting from there, it is only a question of how these minimal consistencies, which the psychoanalyst calls (R), (S), (I), are woven of voice as a fundamental lack in each dimension of a signifier. The voice brings forth speech precisely as something which is not an element in the system. I identify the moebian spatiality of the unconscious to what Euler describes as the functions of the spaces of mouth.[4] This helps us grasp that as it concerns 'body', the holes we cannot avoid to go through and think about have to do with spaces where voice resonates through marks in a jouissance lost to each dimension of (R), (S), (I). My hypothesis is that *'body' exists as a space for a reference to jouissance*, supporting the transmission of castration from one generation to another. To this, I identify the toric structure.[5]

This helps us grasp that the way Lacan situates the experience of identification as an 'internal eight' in regard to the differences between clinical structures is linked to an internal finality of structure.[6] The fact of belonging to the same structure of bispatiality does not lead to scenarios in which the one structure becomes the other, or vice versa. There are moments when, for example, psychosis and obsessional neurosis neighbor each other. Why this happens remains an open question. But still, there is a fundamental difference between clinical structures. The clinic shows the ways a structure is actualizing itself is substantially different between the two.

It seems to me that the word 'ambiguous' is introduced in the place of the fundamental impossibility to experience the jouissance of the mother's body. This has a certain promise, like a hope in the present. Moving the emphasis to consistence helps us explain that what psychoanalysis calls 'body' cannot be reduced to an identity of the subject. This is why it is more precise to say speaking body. It places an emphasis on the fact that the spatialities relevant from the irreducibility of jouissance in its continuums having only to do with how the substance of a subject is realizing itself in subjectivity.

What this means may be expressed as follows: the body cannot be reduced to a thing or an entity. It is only to do with the ways a subject incorporates what lacks in the subject as jouissance in a fantasy. This is why I say sex is above all an invention of body. That is, object choice is only the responsibility of the subject.

It is sure that anxiety is real. How do we know? It is felt in the body without necessarily being able to point exactly to it. Schreber teaches us something else regarding the voice as a real of dimension. There is a form the object induces that remains irreducible to any equivalence. Placing an emphasis on the condition of listening helps us grasp why foreclosures of voice—the non-deployment or extremely partialized extensions of voice in a triple finality—can result in, for example, a continuum of gaze.[7] Schreber experiences an obligation to feminize himself for a look that is permanently fixed. In this way, he tries to make the order of the universe hold together. The symbolic is effectively foreclosed in the aforesaid. The look that is all prevalent and the voice that sounds form an aim.

This does not mean that psychosis is a life condemned to torment and suffering. This is where psychoanalysis offers an option that does not seem to appear in other clinics. When one accepts to be only in the position of a listener, one can also hear the ways improvisations are working for a psychotic subject, enabling a life that does not always suffer by the lack. In the transference, it is also sure that when the subject knows it is heard, something else comes, which is a kind of duty to resituate jouissance. We must not forget here that psychoanalysis is also limited. So, it

76 Formations of voice

would be error here to assume that I am suggesting that psychoanalysis is a kind of possible cure for all or for anyone. It is an alternative to the norm on the basis of a building consistence (knowledge that is never cumulative).

Notes

1 Helene Deutch comes close to this when she speaks of the necessity of the mother to empty herself in order to hear the complaints of the child. Helene Deutsch, *Neuroses and Character Types; Clinical Psychoanalytic Studies* (New York: International University Press, 1965), and Helene Deutsch, *The Psychology of Women: A Psychoanalytic Interpretation* (New York: Grune & Stratton, 1944).
2 To interpretive cuts, I associate the moment when the signifier leaves the signifying movement resulting in a lack in fantasy. And to metaphoric interpretations, I associate interpreting letters leading to a resituating of jouissance.
3 Loenhard Euler, "Thoughts on the Formation of the Voice," *Opera Postuma*, January 1, 1862, https://scholarlycommons.pacific.edu/euler-works/852.
4 Here one finds the 'opening' and 'closing' of the subject of the unconscious/subject of speech.
5 In *L'étourdit*, Lacan conceptualized the passages between the borromean knot and the moebius strip as a torus. Lacan, "L'étourdit," 449–95.
6 Jacques Lacan, "Seminar IX: Identification," trans. Cormac Gallagher, 1961–62 (unpublished).
7 Indeed, one also starts to get ahold of the fact that investigating an *a* like a grammarian or a natural scientist is, in a certain way, experience blind. To borrow from Bruno Bettelheim, such a method cannot avoid involving blinders of narcissism.

Chapter 23

Fourth consistency

The question of the names-of-the-father as a fourth consistency remains open. Subjective topology helps show that it is not a religious concept. It is a principle of authority that continuously inscribes itself as an imperative to have value for any subject. The symbolic phallus Φ is also a metaphor actualizing signifiers of high value, generating the compactifications of the dimensions called R, S, I of the subjective space.

When we move the perspective from an emphasis on the concept to variations that clinical experience shows, it becomes clear that the fourth consistency with which we meet is the symptom. When Lacan discovered the sinthomatic structure, he renewed the question of the symptom.[1] He shows that it is no longer only linked to an unconscious conflict but also to something that has to do with a kind of body event. Situating the symptom in the borromean knot makes more precise what Freud grasps in a much deeper way towards the end of his work in *Inhibitions, Symptoms, and Anxiety*.

Putting the symptom in the knot brings forth, for example, the linkage of the phobic symptom to inhibition and anxiety. There is a difference between signifiers and jouissance and between jouissance and letters. Between the two, there is an inseparability that continuously calls for a subjective separation. The symptom is an instance of an internal transformation of the structure resulting in a knotting. In neurosis, we see that the symptom prevents a covariation among (R), (S), (I). Why? Psychoanalytic experience teaches us that there is a part of the symptom that evades and perplexes. But there is also the 'it's not quite this' or 'this is never quite that'. This part is sustained by infinite forms of satisfaction/dissatisfaction, some of which lie. No doubt, this is one reason why analysis is characterized as slow going and arduous. It can take quite a bit of time to get ahold of and forsake the pretense to an imaginary of variability. The issue a fourth consistency implies is a question of how a signifier is introduced to the law. That is, it is not a matter of a number but of a plurality irreducible to a one of the difference.

As I grasp it, the sinthome is not something created by a psychoanalytic encounter. It is not a supplement. It is a part of the infinite of elements. This helps explain why, for a sinthomatic subject, a symptom can help give stability to the ego. We

DOI: 10.4324/9781003366096-23

are reminded once more that desire cannot be created out of nothing. The four of the knot speaks to listening as the fundamental condition of life. Let us therefore propose that suffering is not the fundamental condition of life, even though experiencing it through frustration, castration, and privation is necessary.

Note

1 Lacan, *The Sinthome*.

Chapter 24

Assumption of nomination

What can it mean to assume a nomination? When Freud speaks about the dissolution of the castration complex, he follows a certain necessity. He grasps that the symptom is not only an expression of the unconscious; it is also something that contains the function of a defense against anxiety. The idea that the form of the symptom plays leaves only a remainder, which exists to the subject as a notion of its content. In effect, it diverts attention to signifiers that are believed to constitute the supposed knowledge of the Other (one of desire and one of demand). The dissolution is characterized by the need to abandon the attempt to derive subjective positions, and the phenomena that appear connected to them, from biological deficiencies or from kinship relations.[1]

In psychoanalysis, sexual difference is experienced by the subject in ways that are sustained by substance in structure (R, S, I). When coordinated by sociological methods, we see that there is a look to culture to define sex and gender. Nomination is not an accident of culture. It is a necessity that has no end or beginning because it is linked to a symbolic nomination of the subject. The ways a subject accepts this necessity and goes about finding forms of satisfaction/dissatisfaction are indeterminate. This also implies a necessity to separate the fantasies of the parents from the subjective needs of the child. It is necessary, in other words, to make a distinction between the types of 'facts' inferred from what presents itself as a true picture of the parental Other and the intentions supposed to it. We cannot say exactly what castration is. It is a question fundamentally open to the subject because it is linked to subjective positions that are, in themselves, in effect of the lack as something which is not an element in the structure. It is sure that 'a woman' is subjected to castration no more nor less than 'a man'. Castration has only to do with how a subject accepts or refuses a part he or she has not. Castration seems suitable to define the indeterminate category of body. This indeterminateness opens a path for a feminine jouissance enabling a subject to experience love beyond object.

To say there exists a jouissance that is outside imagination and felt beyond any image is far from any idealism. Psychoanalytic experience shows that it is possible to construct it in subjectivity, without the possibility of formulations as such. Perhaps realism is better suited since one of the meanings of feminine jouissance is accepting to be limited in order to come to more freedom.

DOI: 10.4324/9781003366096-24

80 Assumption of nomination

Today, the emphasis on speaking in terms of gender shows that what is called 'masculine' or 'feminine' are artifices of social constructions. It is no longer taken for granted that a person's individual dispositions are connected to a sex assigned at birth. Sex and gender are no longer taken to be bodily givens. Now, gender does not define what a person is. This gives a lot of freedom. Psychoanalytically speaking, the difficulty is to *realize how this gives* freedom. These advances imply new interpretations of love. Now, in this moment, love is not referring to a love between sexes but to a love between persons. The question of the changing references of love is not only a question for our culture. It is also a question for psychoanalysis.

Psychoanalysis cannot speak of individualist ideologies. Indeed, such ideologies, linked as they are to choices of object, are outside the field. It is also not the task of psychoanalysis to propose (theoretical or practical) solutions to sociological problems. What follows then?

Psychoanalysis teaches us that it is not an intellectual experience. The internal finality matters in fundamental ways. It is to do with a perception of *the group* of subspaces (body). Euler's formations of voice carries out a difficult philosophical question removed from ideologies of body or any character of beauty and elegance. Without neglecting the details, his formations are a kind of syllogism in effect of elements arranged in such a way that it evokes a feeling of a psychoanalytical law as a law to listen. There is a question of the body made in the image of a myth of 'man'/'woman' as side by side. There is also a question of an *alternating* of elements as calling upon likenesses to the signifiers 'father' and 'mother'. Here is where the philosophical difficulty appears and where psychoanalysis offers a different reply. It is also where Euler arrives at a different place. We use a body in passing through it in the form of metaphors (what he calls 'breathing'). The point to emphasize is that 'breathing', a necessary function of the body, is not reduced to an imaginary of writing. There is a continuous generation of subspaces of jouissance articulated through a triple finality. It is a kind of manifesting of the identification of the subject of speech (the structure of the unconscious) with its topology.

In the experience of the psychoanalytic cure, when a subject comes to a point of castration, the field of possible suddenly open to the subject is the arrangement he or she alone wants. A person can have love, sexuality, sex, body the way they want. But it is very difficult to move to a position substantially separated from perceptions of the Other's demands/desires. Arriving at a point of castration is not only a ridding of the power of the influence of external norms. It also has to do with how the assumption of nomination has an effect of knowledge felt in the absence of religious, social, or transcendent norms. *This knowledge* is an instantiation of a subjective norm. It consists in taking a distance from the demands/desires of the Other, which effectively reduces suffering. This norm is a symbolic normative space. It is not a morality valid for all; it is valid only for the subject. This is what psychoanalysis calls freedom. It is close to what Leibniz deduces from the notion of necessity. There exist 'truths which cannot be reduced by any analysis to identical truths or to the principle of contradiction'.[2]

It is difficult to conceptualize and convey the ends of transference. Subjective experience affirms it in the real of substance.[3] The subject knows that the first substance is not an all-mighty God (or Other) and carries on. Whether or not it stands the test of an objective verification makes no difference. Not all the difficulties have suddenly disappeared. Regarding the 'feminine jouissance', we do not know all its limitations. This is why we are justified in supposing that in a continuum always repeating itself as different to itself, it is possible that the subject can form more different formations than can be imagined. In this sense, 'feminine jouissance' is felt beyond the variability of the imaginary body. The only facts that matter and that make a difference are those that acquaint us with the fundamental lack in the law. It is this that helps sustain us in a capacity of listening and, thus, in an openness towards others. Here, we find the chances of the path that must be selected, that of a right internal one.[4]

Notes

1 Sigmund Freud, "The Dissolution of the Oedipus Complex," in *The Ego and the Id and Other Works: 1923–1925*, ed. and trans. James Strachey, The Standard Edition of the Complete Psychological Works of Sigmund Freud, vol. 19 (London: Vintage, 2001 [1924]), 171–80.
2 Leibniz, "On Body and Force, Against the Cartesians (May 1702)," 250–56. Gottfried Wilhelm Leibniz, "On Freedom (1689?)," in *Philosophical Essays*, trans. Roger Ariew and Daniel Garber (Indianapolis: Hackett Publishing Company, 1989), 94–98, 98.
3 This is what topology, and I would add only topology, brings: it is not a question of abstracting something but an effort of the subject to construct a knowledge and continue building it on the basis of points known and unknown. Indeed, as even mathematical topology demonstrates, such a methodology brings about effects that are, in a sense, the unthought part of philosophy. The knot goes into reality in a way that no longer justifies supposing that absolute space exists. Psychoanalytic experience shows that space as extension does not add anything to body (as Descartes seemed to think) just as time does not add anything to duration. This is why we are justified in saying that the knot is, in the same moment, the support of a subject and the real of the subject.
4 It's what Lacan calls *orthos logos* in *L'étourdit*.

Chapter 25

A return to our psychoanalytical lexicon

Let us return to our psychoanalytical lexicon, summarizing and adding the following:

jouissance: a differential of the movement of signifiers and letters (it is outside any principle of pleasure).

the Other: a circle of close ones, imaginary or symbolic. Lacan's notation $\emptyset$ helps here. It shows the necessity to introduce a signifier.

signifier: an image always goes with it, inducing a reality.

letter: effect of speech in its inseparability from resonances of voice in (R), (S), (I).

voice: echo of a presence that lacks in dimensions (R), (S), (I).

sex: does not define any relation to being, relatively underdetermined.

body: subspaces situating the real of speech in the holes of the knot by generating spaces for jouissance.

nomination: a necessary privation linked to unconscious sayings.

name: ensemble composed of an inseparability of signifiers, letters, jouissance.

one: invariance; a way to characterize structure by a substance.

name: an ensemble of letters woven of marks in a signifier that testify to singularity while helping the subject to situate themselves among others and participate.

Φ: a point of real, supporting how the subject of the unconscious is continuously deploying itself as different to itself.

Ψ: the subject of speech is a real generating knowledge effects (jouissance).

x: a variable, a question of how the object (a) is emerging and where it is appearing.

ω: unconscious perceptions. For the subject, they are a real without meaning and without imaginary (for example, perception of an excess from the presence of the Other such as in anxiety when the subject perceives a demand or a perception of the existence of the Other as lacking being). They are effectively first perceptions insofar as they give the subject a certitude. Unconscious discourse goes towards these perceptions.

Φx: it is impossible as a cause, linked to the necessity to extract signifiers as objects evoking jouissance as present/absent.

Ψx: it is impossible to have all the jouissance in a signifying arrangement; it is linked to the necessity to extract letters metaphorizing missing jouissance.

DOI: 10.4324/9781003366096-25

$\overset{\rightarrow}{\underset{\leftarrow\text{--}}{}}$: it is necessary to fantasize the lack in signifier and to incorporate it *by a lack*.

Taking into account the linkage between sex and nomination as an ongoing covariation of speech and jouissance on the basis of one as an invariance, I propose the following writing of the sexuation of the subject.

$$\frac{\Psi x}{\Phi x} \quad \overset{\rightarrow}{\underset{\leftarrow\text{--}}{}} \quad \omega$$

This is my hypothesis. It is provisional and open to reformulations. I have tried to explain how subjective transformations of sexual difference occur and how they are possible separated from object—since this is what the clinic shows happens. Any errors, inconsistencies, and problems in conveying the subject in simple and precise ways, are to do with the complexities of this subject, which continue to confront us in the unconscious structure of a group.

Acknowledgements

It is not possible to do psychoanalytical work on one's own. I would also like to thank Patricia Gherovici, Nicolas Testé, Jed Wilson, and Marie-Laure Bromley-Davenport for their help. I also thank Ana Pacheco for her help with the figures.

Bibliography

Anzaldúa, Gloria. 1991. *Borderlands: The New Mestiza/La Frontera*. San Francisco: Aunt Lute Books.

Aristotle. 2009a. "Metaphysics." In *The Complete Works of Aristotle. 2*, edited by Jonathan Barnes, translated by W. D. Ross, 1551–1728. Princeton: Princeton University Press.

———. 2009b. "On Marvellous Things Heard." In *The Complete Works of Aristotle. 2*, edited by Jonathan Barnes, translated by L. D. Dowdall, 127298. Princeton: Princeton University Press.

———. 2009c. "Physics." In *The Complete Works of Aristotle. 1*, edited by Jonathan Barnes, translated by R. P. Hardie and R. K. Gaye, 315–446. Princeton: Princeton University Press.

Aulagnier, Piera. 2001. *The Violence of Interpretation: From Pictogram to Statement*. Translated by Alan Sheridan. The New Library of Psychoanalysis 41. London and New York: Routledge.

Bettelheim, Bruno. 1952. *Symbolic Wounds: Puberty Rites and the Envious Male*. New York: Collier Books.

Bion, Wilfred R. 1989. *Elements of Psychoanalysis*. London: Karnac.

Bursztein, Jean-Gérard. 2017a. *Cohérence Philosophique de La Psychanalyse: Aristote, Lacan*. Paris: Hermann.

———. 2017b. *Un lexique de topologie subjective*. Hermann Psychanalyse. Paris: Hermann.

———. 2019. *Psychanalyse et Philosophie Borroméenne*. Paris: Hermann.

Butler, Judith. 1986. "Sex and Gender in Simone de Beauvoir's Second Sex." *Yale French Studies*, no. 72: 35–49.

———. 2004. *Undoing Gender*. New York and London: Routledge.

———. 2011. *Bodies That Matter: On the Discursive Limits of "Sex."* Routledge Classics. New York: Routledge.

Cixous, Hélène. 1976. "The Laugh of the Medusa." Translated by Keith Cohen and Paula Cohen. *Signs* 1 (4): 875–93.

Copjec, Joan. 2015. *Read My Desire: Lacan Against the Historicists*. Radical Thinkers. Cambridge: MIT Press.

Dedekind, Richard. 1963. *Essays on the Theory of Numbers: I. Continuity and Irrational Numbers. II. The Nature and Meaning of Numbers*. New York: Dover Publications.

Derrida, Jacques. 1998. *Of Grammatology*. Translated by Gayatri Chakravorty Spivak. Baltimore: Johns Hopkins University Press.

86   Bibliography

Deutsch, Helene. 1944. *The Psychology of Women: A Psychoanalytic Interpretation*. New York: Grune & Stratton.

———. 1965. *Neuroses and Character Types: Clinical Psychoanalytic Studies*. New York: International University Press.

Euler, Leonhard. 1862. "Meditatio de Formatione Vocum." *Opera Postuma*. January 1, 1862. https://scholarlycommons.pacific.edu/euler-works/852.

Foucault, Michel. 1988a. *The History of Sexuality: Vol 2: The Use of Pleasure*. Translated by Robert Hurley. New York: Vintage Books.

———. 1988b. *The History of Sexuality: Vol I: An Introduction*. Translated by Robert Hurley. New York: Vintage Books.

Freud, Sigmund. (1905) 2001h. "Fragment of an Analysis of a Case of Hysteria (1905 [1901])." In *A Case of Hysteria, Three Essays on Sexuality and Other Works: (1901–1905)*, edited and translated by James Strachey, 1–122. The Standard Edition of the Complete Psychological Works of Sigmund Freud, Vol. 7. London: Vintage.

———. (1905) 2001s. "Three Essays on the Theory of Sexuality." In *A Case of Hysteria, Three Essays on Sexuality and Other Works; (1901–1905)*, edited and translated by James Strachey, 123–246. The Standard Edition of the Complete Psychological Works of Sigmund Freud, Vol. 7. London: Vintage.

———. (1909) 2001b. "Analysis of a Phobia in a Five-Year-Old Boy." In *Two Case Histories: "Little Hans" and the "Rat Man" (1909)*, edited and translated by James Strachey, 1–150. The Standard Edition of the Complete Psychological Works of Sigmund Freud, Vol. 10. London: Vintage.

———. (1913) 2001t. "Totem and Taboo: Some Points of Agreement between the Mental Lives of Savages and Neurotics (1913 [1912–13])." In *Totem and Taboo and Other Works: 1913–1914*, edited and translated by James Strachey, vii–162. The Standard Edition of the Complete Psychological Works of Sigmund Freud, Vol. 13. London: Vintage.

———. (1915) 2001r. "The Unconscious." In *On the History of the Psychoanalytic Movement, Papers on Metapsychology and Other Works (1914–1916)*, edited and translated by James Strachey, Vol. 14:159–214. The Standard Edition of the Complete Psychological Works of Sigmund Freud. London: Vintage.

———. (1918) 2001i. "From the History of an Infantile Neurosis." In *An Infantile Neurosis and Other Works: 1917–1919*, edited and translated by James Strachey, 1–124. The Standard Edition of the Complete Psychological Works of Sigmund Freud, Vol. 17. London: Vintage.

———. (1919) 2001a " 'A Child is Being Beaten' A Contribution to the Study of the Origin of Sexual Perversions." In *An Infantile Neurosis and Other Works: 1917–1919*, edited and translated by James Strachey, 175–204. The Standard Edition of the Complete Psychological Works of Sigmund Freud, Vol. 17. London: Vintage.

———. (1920) 2001d. "Beyond the Pleasure Principle." In *Beyond the Pleasure Principle: Group Psychology and Other Works: (1920–1922)*, edited and translated by James Strachey, 1–6. The Standard Edition of the Complete Psychological Works of Sigmund Freud, Vol. 18. London: Vintage.

———. (1920) 2001q. "The Psychogenesis of a Case of Homosexuality in a Woman." In *Beyond the Pleasure Principle, Group Psychology and Other Works: (1920–1922)*, edited and translated by James Strachey, 145–72. The Standard Edition of the Complete Psychological Works of Sigmund Freud, Vol. 18. London: Vintage.

———. (1921) 2001j. "Group Psychology and the Analysis of the Ego." In *Beyond the Pleasure Principle, Group Psychology and Other Works: (1920–1922)*, edited and translated by James Strachey, 65–144. The Standard Edition of the Complete Psychological Works of Sigmund Freud, Vol. 18. London: Vintage.

———. (1923) 2001o. "The Ego and the Id." In *The Ego and the Id and Other Works: 1923–1925*, edited and translated by James Strachey, 1–66. The Standard Edition of the Complete Psychological Works of Sigmund Freud, Vol. 19. London: Vintage.

———. (1923) 2001p. "The Infantile Genital Organization (An Interpolation into the Theory of Sexuality)." In *The Ego and the Id and Other Works: 1923–1925*, edited and translated by James Strachey, 139–46. The Standard Edition of the Complete Psychological Works of Sigmund Freud, Vol. 19. London: Vintage.

———. (1924) 2001n. "The Dissolution of the Oedipus Complex." In *The Ego and the Id and Other Works: 1923–1925*, edited and translated by James Strachey, 171–80. The Standard Edition of the Complete Psychological Works of Sigmund Freud, Vol. 19. London: Vintage.

———. (1925) 2001m. "Negation." In *The Ego and the Id and Other Works: 1923–1925*, edited and translated by James Strachey, 233–40. The Standard Edition of the Complete Psychological Works of Sigmund Freud, Vol. 19. London: Vintage.

———. (1926) 2001k. "Inhibitions, Symptoms and Anxiety." In *An Autobiographical Study, Inhibitions, Symptoms and Anxiety, The Question of Lay Analysis and Other Works: (1925–1926)*, edited and translated by James Strachey, 75–176. The Standard Edition of the Complete Psychological Works of Sigmund Freud, Vol. 20. London: Vintage.

———. (1927) 2001g. "Fetishism." In *The Future of an Illusion: Civilization and Its Discontent and Other Works: (1927–1931)*, edited and translated by James Strachey, 149–57. The Standard Edition of the Complete Psychological Works of Sigmund Freud, Vol. 21. London: Vintage.

———. (1931) 2001e. "Female Sexuality." In *The Future of an Illusion: Civilization and Its Discontents and Other Works:(1927–1931)*, edited and translated by James Strachey, 221–44. The Standard Edition of the Complete Psychological Works of Sigmund Freud, Vol. 21. London: Vintage.

———. (1933) 2001f. "Femininity." In *New Introductory Lectures on Psychoanalysis and Other Works: (1932–1936)*, edited and translated by James Strachey, 112–35. The Standard Edition of the Complete Psychological Works of Sigmund Freud, Vol. 22. London: Vintage.

———. (1937) 2001c. "Analysis Terminable and Interminable." In *Moses and Monotheism: An Outline of Psychoanalysis and Other Works: (1937–1939)*, edited and translated by James Strachey, 209–54. The Standard Edition of the Complete Psychological Works of Sigmund Freud, Vol. 23. London: Vintage.

———. (1939) 2001l. "Moses and Monotheism: Three Essays." In *Moses and Monotheism, An Outline of Psychoanalysis and Other Works: (1937–1939)*, edited and translated by James Strachey, 1–138. The Standard Edition of the Complete Psychological Works of Sigmund Freud, Vol. 23. London: Vintage.

Gödel, Kurt. 1992. *On Formally Undecidable Propositions of Principia Mathematica and Related Systems*. Translated by B. Meltzer. New York: Dover Publications.

Halberstam, Jack. 2018. *Female Masculinity*. Durham: Duke University Press.

Irigaray, Luce. 1985. *This Sex Which Is Not One*. Translated by Catherine Porter. Ithaca: Cornell University Press.

Jekels, Ludwig. 1941. "Psycho-Analysis and Dialectic." *Psychoanalytic Review* 28: 228–53.

Kripke, Saul A. 1980. *Naming and Necessity*. Cambridge: Harvard University Press.

Kristeva, Julia. 2001. *Female Genius. 1: Hannah Arendt*. Translated by Ross Guberman. New York: Columbia University Press.

88 Bibliography

———. 2004. *Melanie Klein*. Translated by Ross Guberman. New York: Columbia University Press.

Lacan, Jacques. 1961. "Seminar IX: Identification." Translated by Cormac Gallagher. unpublished.

———. 1971. "The Knowledge of the Psychoanalyst: Seven Talks at Sainte-Anne." Translated by Cormac Gallagher. unpublished.

———. 1974. "Seminar XXII: RSI." Translated by Cormac Gallagher. unpublished.

———. 1976. "Seminar XXIV: L'insu Que Sait." Translated by Cormac Gallagher. unpublished.

———. 1990. *Television: A Challenge to the Psychoanalytic Establishment*. Edited by Joan Copjec. Translated by Denis Hollier. New York: W.W. Norton & Company.

———. 1997. *The Psychoses 1955–1956*. Edited by Jacques-Alain Miller. Translated by Russell Grigg, The Seminar of Jacques Lacan, Book III. New York: W.W. Norton & Company.

———. 1998. *The Four Fundamental Concepts of Psychoanalysis*. Edited by Jacques-Alain Miller. Translated by Alan Sheridan. The Seminar of Jacques Lacan, Book XI. New York: W.W. Norton & Company.

———. 1999. *On Feminine Sexuality: The Limits of Love and Knowledge*. Edited by Jacques-Alain Miller. Translated by Bruce Fink, The Seminar of Jacques Lacan, Book XX. New York: W. W. Norton & Company.

———. 2001. "L'étourdit." In *Autres Écrits*, 449–95. Le Champ Freudien. Paris: Editions du Seuil.

———. 2006a. "Seminar on 'The Purloined Letter.'" In *Écrits: The First Complete Edition in English*, translated by Bruce Fink, 6–48. New York: W. W. Norton & Company.

———. 2006b. "The Instance of the Letter in the Unconscious, or Reason Since Freud." In *Écrits: The First Complete Edition in English*, translated by Bruce Fink, 412–41. New York: W.W. Norton & Company.

———. 2007. *The Other Side of Psychoanalysis*. Edited by Jacques-Alain MIller. Translated by Russell Grigg. The Seminar of Jacques Lacan, Book XVII. New York: W.W Norton & Company.

———. 2016a. *Anxiety*. Edited by Jacques-Alain Miller. Translated by A. R. Price, The Seminar of Jacques Lacan, Book X. Cambridge: Polity.

———. 2016b. *The Sinthome*. Edited by Jacques-Alain Miller. Translated by A. R. Price. The Seminar of Jacques Lacan, Book XXIII. Cambridge: Polity.

———. 2017. *Formations of the Unconscious*. Edited by Jacques-Alain Miller. Translated by Russell Grigg. The Seminar of Jacques Lacan, Book V. Malden: Polity.

———. 2018. *Or Worse . . . .* Edited by Jacques-Alain Miller. Translated by A. R. Price. The Seminar of Jacques Lacan, Book XIX. Cambridge: Polity.

Leibniz, Gottfried Wilhelm. 1989a. "On Body and Force, Against the Cartesians (May 1702)." In *Philosophical Essays*, translated by Roger Ariew and Daniel Garber, 250–56. Indianapolis: Hackett Pub. Co.

———. 1989b. "On Freedom (1689?)." In *Philosophical Essays*, translated by Roger Ariew and Daniel Garber, 94–98. Indianapolis: Hackett Pub. Co.

———. 1989c. "On the Nature of Body and the Laws of Motion (ca 1678–82)." In *Philosophical Essays*, translated by Roger Ariew and Daniel Garber, 245–49. Indianapolis: Hackett Pub. Co.

Poincaré, Henri. 1952. *Science and Method*. New York: Dover Publications.

Schreber, Daniel Paul. 2000. *Memoirs of My Nervous Illness*. Translated by Ida Macalpine and Richard A. Hunter. New York: New York Review Books.

Winnicott, D. W. 1954. "Transitional Objects and Transitional Phenomena—A Study of the First Not-Me Possession." *International Journal of Psychoanalysis* 34: 89–97.

Wittgenstein, Ludwig. 1999. *Tractatus Logico-Philosophicus*. Translated by C. K. Ogden. Mineola: Dover Publications.

Wittig, Monique. 1992. *The Straight Mind and Other Essays*. Translated by Marlene Wildeman. Boston: Beacon Press.

Index

Note: Page numbers followed by "n" with numbers refer to notes.

absolute jouissance 19, 50
'A Child is Being Beaten' (Freud) 7, 25, 26, 27n5
all-phallic space 15, 51–5, 61, 66
analytic experience 8n3, 71
antimonies 14, 38
anxiety 53, 59, 75, 79; dimensions of space 60; hysteria of 43; phobic symptom 77; unconscious 43
Ariman 68
Aristotle 3n7, 17n7, 21n1, 25, 27n3
authority principle 11, 77
autoeroticism 30–1
axioms 53

de Beauvoir, Simone 24n3
'being true' 16, 19n2
biological sex 23
Bion, Wilfred R. 3n8, 41; *Elements of Psychoanalysis* 42n9
bispatiality 51, 52, 75
body 65, 82; emergence of 57; and gender 15; ideologies of 80; jouissance of 52, 56; maternal body 39, 51; of the other sex 40; phallic jouissance 23; physical body 30; speaking body 4, 63; subjective perception of 60
borromean 2, 4, 7, 65, 69; structure of metaphor 2, 54, 65; structure of the unconscious 1, 3n1, 4, 8, 16, 16n2, 42n5, 51, 53, 55n3, 55n5, 70
boy/girl 14, 56–7; maternal investment 28–9; nomination of 56; sex, maternal Other 27

Bursztein, Jean-Gérard 1, 3n2, 51; *Psychanalyse et Philosophie Borroméenne* 8n16; *Un lexique de topologie Subjective* 16n2
Butler, Judith 24n1, 24n3

castration (complex) 79–80; different modalities of 51–2; moment of castration when 'space is filled by lack of' 42n5; traditional object existing through, and jouissance 39; transmitted from one generation to another 15;
child 25; axioms 53; fantasy and sex 26; maternal investment 28–9; mother-child tie 61, 70; unconscious knowledge of 70
choice of object 43
clinical structures 41, 75
conscious/unconscious thinking 1–2, 4–8, 10, 14, 26
continuation, hypothesis of 53
conversion, hysteria of 43
Copjec, Joan 24n1
cultural sex 23
cut concept 1, 5

Dedekind, Richard 1, 3n3
deferred action 44, 45
Der ewige Jude (Eternal Jew) 67
Derrida, Jacques 42n6; *Of Grammatology* 42n6
Deutch, Helene 76n1
differential 27, 31, 40, 41, 41n4, 45, 61, 63–4, 69, 73, 82

Index   91

ego 40, 77; anxiety, subjective necessity 53; ideal ego *vs.* ego ideal 2, 6; signifier and jouissance 68; symbolic nomination 30
The Ego and the ID and Other Works (Freud) 8n8, 21n2
ego ideal 2, 6, 44, 48
elements 41, 42n9, 47, 49, 80: imaginary 27, 31; of lack 51, 66; symbolic 27
Elements of Psychoanalysis (Bion) 42n9
envy and envy in excess 65–6
epistemology 4, 5, 34
erotic-abject object 48
eroticism 23
Euler, Loenhard 74–5, 76n3, 80

false reduction 73
fantasy 5–7, 10, 25–8, 37, 56; *choice of object* 43; erotic-abject object 48; masochistic fantasy 49; organization of 58; parental fantasies 7; transmission of 28
fear 60, 61
feminine 51, 59, 80; jouissance 21, 79–81; sexuality 20
femininity 20, 62
feminist philosophy 23
Fetishism (Freud) 58
forbidden jouissance 28
forced choice 19, 28
The Four Fundamental Concepts of Psychoanalysis (Lacan) 8n12
fourth consistency 77–8
Freud, Sigmund 1, 3n6, 18, 20, 33n3, 62, 71; analysis finite and infinite 13n1; castration complex 79; 'A Child is Being Beaten' 7, 25; *The Ego and the ID and Other Works* 8n8, 21n2; *einziger Zug* 5; epistemology 34; *Fetishism* 58; forced choice 19, 28; identification 26; infantile sexuality 25, 34; *Inhibitions, Symptoms, and Anxiety* 60, 77; *Introductory Lectures on Psychoanalysis* 34; *Moses and Monotheism* 18; oedipal sexuality 43; Oedipus complex 67; phallic function 39; psychoanalytic truth 5; reality principle 28; *Totem and Taboo* 18; unterschied and verschiedenheit 20; work on neurosis 2
fundamental disappearance 70
fundamental fantasy 6, 40, 43, 47, 71

gender 54, 59; culture and politics 23; masculine/feminine 80; nomination 79; philosophies of 22; psychoanalysis 53; and sex 3, 5, 14, 22; socio-cultural organization 14, 25, 45; unconscious nomination 15; voice, formations of 73
gender theory 23
Gödel, Kurt 55n4

heteros 7, 9n14, 66
hole 4, 7, 9n14, 23, 25, 27, 27n4, 30, 43, 52, 54, 56, 57, 61, 64, 70, 74–5
homosexuality, in a woman (Freud) 65
hylomorphism 40
hypothesis 48, 67, 72; hypotheses non fingere 52
hysteria/ hysterical 43, 48–9; fantasy 48; symptom 48–50

ideal ego 2, 6
idealism 59, 79
imaginary 6, 7, 15, 22, 30; conscious/ unconscious thinking 26; consistency 26; dimension 30; elements 31; genealogy 18; image 49; interpretation 61; irreducibility of 57; nomination 56, 67; object 74; phallus 71
impossibility notion 35, 46, 50
infantile sexuality 5, 25, 34, 37, 52, 73
infinite 2, 5, 8n3, 15, 17n7, 21, 29, 37–8, 44, 47, 49, 64, 68, 72–3, 77
infinite straight line 37–9, 42n5
inhibition 59, 61, 77
Inhibitions, Symptoms, and Anxiety (Freud) 60, 77
The Instance of the Letter in the Unconscious (Lacan) 70
'internal eight' (Lacan) 75–6, 76n6
interpretation, difficulty of 37–41
Introductory Lectures on Psychoanalysis (Freud) 34
Irigaray, Luce 24n4; *This Sex Which is Not One* 24n4

Jekels, Ludwig 8n9
jealousy 65
jouissance 30–33, 34–7, 48–50; in all-phallic space 52; of body 52, 56; definition of 11, 37; irreducibility of 75; of logos 56; man *vs.* woman 20;

masochistic jouissance 26; missing jouissance 16, 40, 45; modality of 54; movements of 64; names-of-the-father 19; within neurotic structure 49; phallic jouissance 26, 39; psychoanalytic letter 22; of speech 50; subject's jouissance 41; subject woven 25; transformations of 1; unconscious field of 2

kinship 2, 19n1, 79
Kripke, Saul 17n3; *Naming and Necessity* 17n3

Lacan, Jacques 1, 2, 4, 18, 71; borromean structure 16; epistemology 5; *On Feminine Sexuality: The Limits of Love and Knowledge* 8n2; *Formations of the Unconscious: The Seminar of Jacques Lacan* 36n1; *The Four Fundamental Concepts of Psychoanalysis* 8n12; *The Instance of the Letter in the Unconscious* 70; *L'étourdit* 54, 76n5; matheme for sexuation 64; phallic function 39; point at infinity 37; sexuation, formula of 53; sexuation, matheme of 24n1, 44; subjective topology 3n1; substance jouissante 58; *unary trait* 5
language 32–3, 45, 48, 49, 62, 72; deferred action 44; retroactive effect of 52
law of prohibition of incest/law of the unconscious 17, 38, 44, 50
Leibniz, Wilhelm 64
lesbian phallus concept 24n1, 66
letter/letters 20–3, 31, 41, 56–9, 82; definition of 12
lexicon 10–13, 82–3
libidinal position 2
libido 20
logical system/systems 18, 53
logos, jouissance of 56

man/woman 14, 44, 52, 56
masculine 51, 66, 74, 80
masochism 43
masochistic jouissance 26, 48, 50
maternal: body 38, 39, 51, 53, 57; investment 28–9; love 16; nomination 32; phallus 39; speech 44

metaphor 21; definition of 12
metaphoric interpretations 73
moebian spatiality 75; representation of the unconscious 42n5; structure of the unconscious 1, 3n1, 4, 8, 16, 16n2, 42n5, 51, 53, 55n3, 55n5, 70
Moses and Monotheism (Freud) 18
mother: child jouissance 23; definition of 12

names-of-the-father 18–19, 23, 54, 77; definition of 12; deployment of 16
narcissism 44, 48; unconscious image of 35, 44, 60
narcissistic value 49
neighborhood notion 58
neurosis 2, 5, 41
neurotic subject 14
neurotic symptoms 43
nomination 82; assumption of 79–81; fantasy, transmission of 28, 41; gender theory 23; imaginary nomination 56, 67; maternal nomination 32; names/names-of-the-father 16; necessary privation process 15; psychoanalytical concept of 1; redoubling of 31, 35; and sex 14–16, 40, 72; speech of the maternal Other 34; symbolic nomination 19, 30–3, 56; transmission of structure 25; unconscious, borromean knot structure of 4; unconscious nomination 14–15
non-all phallic spaces 51–5, 52, 61
non-existent body 57
non-existent jouissance 39
normative power 47

object 2, 4–7; modalities of 73; of psychoanalysis 14
obligation principle 31
Oedipal sexuality 43
Oedipus complex 18, 25, 43, 67
On Feminine Sexuality: The Limits of Love and Knowledge (Lacan) 8n2
ordinary psychosis 69
Other 39, 45, 82; definition of 12; demands/desires of 71; erotic-abject object 48; jouissance of 43; knowledge of 79; in psychosis 68
other sex 14, 20, 23, 28, 35, 40, 54, 56

paranoia 65, 67
paternal function 21, 50; definition of 12
penis envy 38, 62, 65
phallic function 19, 20, 38, 39, 56, 64
phallic jouissance 23, 26, 39, 49, 61
phallus 20, 22, 23
philosophical approaches 22
physical principle 62
plurality 24, 26, 54, 68, 77
Poincaré, Henri 37
power 6, 10, 23, 47, 54, 73, 80
principle mechanism 43
privilege 18, 57
prohibition principle 45
proximities 74
Psychanalyse et Philosophie Borroméenne
 (Bursztein) 8n16
psychoanalysis: body 75; definition of
 19n1; freedom 80; individuals,
 social roles 22; infantile sexuality
 37; language 72; letter 74;
 mathematical knowledge 2;
 objectivism 34; organ 30; the penis
 62; phallus 22, 23, 35; sex and
 gender 53; sexual difference 79;
 sexual relation 16; and topology
 1, 4
psychoanalytic/psychoanalytical: cure 80;
 experience 6, 10, 23, 25, 30, 46, 61,
 77, 79; formations 74; group 46–7;
 imaginary modal 6; interpretations
 1, 10; invariance 5, 22–4;
 knowledge 11; letter 22; lexicon
 11, 13n2, 82–3; symbolic modal
 6; terminology 11; theory 4; truth
 2–3, 5, 37, 73; work 13; writing 72
psychosis 41, 68, 69
psychotic structure 69
psychotic subject 14
The Purloined Letter 70

radical alternative 14, 41, 67–9
rationality 34, 37
reality: definition of 28; principle of 28
real of the imaginary 7, 30, 63, 74
real of the real 7, 63, 74
real of the symbolic 7
religious concept 77
repression 8n8, 23, 34, 43, 53, 56–57,
 60–2, 67, 70–1; principle of 26,
 43, 45, 70; return of repression 22,
 67, 69

resemblance 69
resituate jouissance 40

same space 20, 50, 51, 53
satisfaction/dissatisfaction 77
Schreber, Daniel Paul 67–8, 75
self 2, 43; self-discovery 10
semblant: of body 43–5; definition of 12
sex: biological sex 23; cultural sex 23; and
 gender philosophies 3, 5, 14, 22;
 nomination 22, 35, 40; one sex
 20–1, 72; opposite sex 26; other
 sex 20, 26, 52; social sex 23; socio-
 cultural organization 14, 25, 45;
 unconscious nomination 15
sexual code 22, 28
sexual difference 2, 3, 18, 25, 44,
 67–9, 79
sexuality 21, 45; feminine sexuality 20;
 infantile sexuality 5, 25, 34,
 52, 73; oedipal sexuality 43;
 psychoanalysis speak 34
sexual relation 16, 51
sexuation 21, 22, 45, 83; formula of 53;
 matheme of 24n1, 44
signifiers 60–2, 82; definition of 11, 52;
 jouissance linked to 65; parental
 context 63; remark in 70–1;
 transmission of 35
simplicity 37
singularity, definition of 6
sinthome 8n3, 41n3, 77–8, 78n1;
 sinthomatic structure 77; and
 sinthomatic subject 77
social dynamics 10
social sex 23
socio-cultural objects 25
socio-cultural organization 14
sociological methods 79
somatic compliance 43
soul-voluptuousness feeling 68
source, lost/loss of 41
space, dimensions of 8
speaking body 4, 63; definition 4
speech: jouissances 50; maternal speech
 44; structure of 56; subject of 5,
 12, 15, 42n11, 63, 64, 76n4, 80, 82;
 transmission of 64; unconscious 41
structure transmission 41
subject: definition of 11; meanings of 1
subjective deductions 64
subjective knowledge 11, 50

94 Index

subjective position 2, 21, 31, 35, 45, 47, 52, 57, 58, 61, 73, 79; position of listener 72, 73, 75; positions of signifier 13, 52, 58, 73; position of speech 58, 72, 73, 74, 75; separated from object 39, 52, 57, 63
subjective separation 77
subjective topology 1–3, 27, 37, 41, 46, 49, 59, 63, 66, 77; unconscious, spatiality of 2
subjectivity 15, 25, 28, 34
substance 3n1, 3n7, 4, 12, 14, 21, 22, 25, 38, 42n6, 58, 63, 69, 74, 79, 80–1
substance jouissante 4, 58, 63
surplus image 49
symbolic 7; dimension 49; elements 31; modal 6; nomination 19, 30–3, 56–7; phallus 4, 23, 29, 35, 41, 77; value 35, 49
symptom 60–2

thickness/thinness 74
time, concept of 73
topology 1–4, 20, 27, 37, 41, 46, 49, 58, 63, 81n3
torus 76n5
Totem and Taboo (Freud) 18
Tractatus Logico-Philosophicus (Wittgenstein) 8n6, 19n3
transformation law 31
transitional object 26–7
trauma 35

tridimensionality 4, 24, 44, 49, 59
truth 6, 7, 38, 80; principle of contradiction 80; psychoanalytical truth 2, 5, 37

unary trait 54, 63
unconscious: anxiety 43; borromean knot 2, 4, 7, 16; continuum hypothesis of 52; expression of 79; moebian structure of 51; moebian spatiality of 75; narcissism image 7; nomination 15; sexuation 20; speech 41; subject woven 25; symbolic elements 31; symbolic law of 44; symbolic nomination 30; topological structure of 1, 8, 51, 70
unity, fusional feeling of 60
Un lexique de topologie Subjective (Bursztein) 16n2

voice, formations of 72–6, 82
voluptuousness 68

weaving principle 11
Winnicott, D. W. 26, 39
Wittgenstein, Ludwig 44; Tractatus Logico-Philosophicus 8n6, 19n3
Wittig, Monique 24n4
women 57; body of 45, 49; homosexuality in 65; non-all phallic space 51; Oedipus complex 19; penis envy to 62; psychoanalysis 30; signifiers 43–5; situation of lack in 30